30 Days
of
Gratitude

The Gratitude Program That Will Change Your Life

JULIE BOYER

BALBOA.
PRESS

A DIVISION OF HAY HOUSE

Balboa Press books may be ordered through booksellers or by contacting:

Balboa Press
A Division of Hay House
1663 Liberty Drive
Bloomington, IN 47403
www.balboapress.com
1-(877) 407-4847

Because of the dynamic nature of the Internet, any web addresses or links contained in this book may have changed since publication and may no longer be valid. The views expressed in this work are solely those of the author and do not necessarily reflect the views of the publisher, and the publisher hereby disclaims any responsibility for them.

The author of this book does not dispense medical advice or prescribe the use of any technique as a form of treatment for physical, emotional, or medical problems without the advice of a physician, either directly or indirectly. The intent of the author is only to offer information of a general nature to help you in your quest for emotional and spiritual well-being. In the event you use any of the information in this book for yourself, which is your constitutional right, the author and the publisher assume no responsibility for your actions.

Any people depicted in stock imagery provided by Thinkstock are models, and such images are being used for illustrative purposes only. Certain stock imagery © Thinkstock.

Printed in the United States of America.

ISBN: 978-1-4525-7272-7 (sc)
ISBN: 978-1-4525-7273-4 (e)

Balboa Press rev. date: 05/07/2013

Table of Contents

For printable worksheets and other useful forms to download please visit: www.30daysofgratitudebook.com

This book is dedicated to my beautiful daughter, Céline.

I am forever grateful that God blessed us with
your incredible spirit.

Acknowledgements

This book was a labour of love by an incredible team of people. I am deeply grateful for all of the wonderful people who helped me bring this book into reality. To my sister, Sophie, who was my editor, I am most grateful. I always knew she was a talented writer and editor, but we never had the chance to work together on a project. She helped make my writing more concise and my ideas clearer. I learned a lot from working with her, and it has been one of the best things I have shared with my sister.

To one of my best friends and mentor, Leanne Grechulk, who wrote the Forward for this book, I am grateful for all of her wisdom, kindness, generosity, forgiveness and love. My life is forever changed because she is a part of it, and that is a blessing.

To my parents, Louise and Jérôme, who always support me, no matter what non-traditional path I choose. They have given me the gifts of love and affection, persistence and determination, and a passion for life. Je vous remercie du fond de mon cœur.

To Denis Waitley, for believing in me, inspiring me, and shining a light on those that surround him. Thank you.

To my incredible team, I am honoured to work with all of you every single day and grateful for all you have taught me. I am thrilled by your successes and rooting for you every step of the way. I am so grateful for everyone who is a part of Game Changers International, so many of you have inspired me to be the best person I can be.

To the team from Balboa Press, you have exceeded my expectations and I am grateful to have chosen to align with your team to publish my first book.

To all of my mentors, living or not, whether I have met them or not, I am grateful. It is the wisdom I have learned from all of them that I shared in this book.

And finally to my husband Dan and daughter Céline. We are a family and that is what is most important to me above all else. Your support, patience and love are what allowed me to finish this book and share my message with the world. Thank you for being the most important people in my world. I am grateful to have been blessed with the perfect family.

Forward

When one feels gratitude, life is bliss. In a constant state of overstimulation, overdrive and chaos, it can be challenging to stay connected and present. I am grateful for my daily yoga practice and Hay House for helping me get back to centre. My dear friend Julie has given us simple steps and strategies for reconnecting with our true self. When we are grateful, life simply works better, flows more freely and we bring more joy to the world. I am certain that the contrast between light and dark in our daily lives helps us to connect with the feeling of gratitude. At the same time, this contrast challenges us to remain grateful in our hearts on those darker days. It is easy to journal a lists of things, experiences and people we are grateful for, but Julie reminds us that the key is connection; connecting to our hearts and to the feeling of gratitude is truly miraculous.

Over the past few years, Julie has inspired me to dig deeper and experience gratitude at a much more profound level. We can all think gratitude (in our minds), but it is the feeling of it (in our hearts) that bring tears to our eyes. When we truly feel gratitude, every cell in our body smiles; it allows us to feel pure joy, and encourages us to serve on a global scale. The irony is that feeling gratitude permits us to be divinely happy for the little moments in our lives, yet makes us want to give more, share more and connect more. I genuinely believe that you will be much more connected to your true authentic self by reading this book. Julie has an incredible ability to distill the simple daily steps for us that, when applied, will lead to massive shifts in our lives. Her daily exercises and wisdom have not only helped me connect my head to my heart on most days, but it has also encouraged me to practice vulnerability.

The most important time in our lives to practice gratitude is when things aren't going the way we want, expect or intend. These times in our lives are our teachers; our teachers for patience, gratitude and love. If you are going through a challenging time in your life right now, reading this book will guide you through your transition, and remind you that the true gift is being able to love your life and yourself. Being grateful in tough times is also a challenge, as our mind constantly wants to take over our lives and our hearts. Julie reminds and teaches us that gratitude keeps our lives flowing, our hearts soaring and our souls smiling.

In our busy lives, it is a challenge to stay connected, grounded and in a state of love and gratitude. It is essential to find constant guidance and support from many incredible teachers. Julie has been a blessing in many areas of my life, but her book has helped me incredibly as I transition to my new role in this world as a mother. What I love most about her book is its simplicity, authenticity and energy. She is truly with you on each page and throughout your journey. I am grateful for every inch of my journey thus far, even the darker days. When I allow myself to get caught up with the busiest days it is so easy to live in my mind and forget about my heart. This book is about living gratitude, not just thinking it. I am grateful for this book as a gentle and loving reminder that our journey on this earth is but a brief moment... and I want to savour every breath.

Walk as if you are kissing the Earth with your feet
—Thich Nhat Hanh

Leanne Grechulk, seeker, student, teacher
www.leannegrechulk.com

Introduction

Why *30 Days of Gratitude*? What exactly can be accomplished in only thirty days? This book was written to share with you some of the most powerful and effective gratitude habits that I have learned through personal challenges, successes, and failures. It is a straightforward guide that will help you discover how to live in a state of gratitude, creating daily gratitude habits so that you can attract everything your heart desires— and more. Alongside gratitude, you'll learn about the importance of allowing abundance into your life, and the role of faith in creating the life of your dreams. My gift is to inspire you to take daily action, which will lead to small, positive changes in your life; over time, perhaps you'll have created an entirely new life for yourself!

To start off, what are the benefits to living your life with a grateful mindset? There are a few obvious ones that come to mind: a positive outlook, better relationships, more success and abundance. What you may not realize is that living from a place of daily gratitude not only changes your own life, but can influence the lives of those around you. You may even find that you are surrounding yourself with different people, and participating in new and diverse activities as you work your way through this book. It's not important where you are right now, it's all about the journey, and the more risks you are willing to take as you read through *30 Days of Gratitude*, the more powerful the reward. Push the limits of your comfort zone; even if you feel fear or discomfort, keep going. Find out what awaits you on the other side!

Before we get into the daily lessons, I'd like to share my story with you, so that you can understand the challenges I've faced, and see how gratitude changed my life over the course of a few short years. Just over a decade ago, both my marriage and my contract at a large blue-chip company were ending. Times were tough, but I took this as an opportunity to start over again in many ways. I had the chance to work overseas, and spent over two years working in Switzerland, living in the mountains. I even spent two winters skiing in the Alps. I was in an amazing place, with incredible opportunities, so you would think I would be grateful every single day. And there were definitely moments of gratitude—such as the first time I hiked up to the top of a glacier or when I learned how to ski off-piste in knee-deep powder—but I would have to admit that I didn't live from a place of gratitude daily. In fact, there were many times when I acted out of a sense of entitlement and was ruled by my emotions. I am not always proud of the way I acted. My reactions would have been quite different had I been acting from a place of gratitude.

There were many times when I reacted personally to situations that had nothing to do with me (leading with my ego) and used emotional blackmail to get what I wanted. I also found that I was often the outsider, trying to fit in. My self-talk could be very negative, and I realize now that I created these situations myself by making assumptions about what others thought of me. And when you are living from emotion and choosing to listen to negative self-talk, it's easy to see why fitting in with others might not be that simple. And finally, I found it very hard to be excited or grateful for other people's successes. Being a naturally competitive person I didn't understand that another person's success takes absolutely nothing away from me and my own unlimited possibilities of success. This scarcity mentality would continue to linger for many years after and almost caused me to lose my business and my best friends.

When I returned from my time overseas, I was given an incredible opportunity to start my own business while working with some of my best friends. I was blessed to have a mentor in Leanne Grechulk, who saw greatness in me long before I could see it for myself. During the first few years, it was very challenging both from a financial standpoint and also because of a steep learning curve. I had always wanted to be an entrepreneur and own my own business as I had never been a great employee. Yet I knew nothing about the industry I had chosen and even less about the personal development necessary to be successful. My first introduction on this incredible journey was through the movie version of The Secret. After watching this film over a dozen times, I started on my own personal development journey, all the while building a business and doing whatever it took to make ends meet, including cashing in my retirement savings and starting up a second business at the same time to create more cash flow.

Two years later and it was clear (to me) that I was the Superstar. I achieved new levels more quickly than anyone else at that time, I won awards several years in a row and I was a (self-appointed) **Leader**. It took me a few more years and several more John C. Maxwell books before I realized what a true leader looks like. Yet, no matter how much money I made, no matter how many awards I won and trainings I lead, I was never satisfied. I could never simply be grateful or happy. I was always looking ahead to the next goal or the next level. Despite my accomplishments and being surrounded by a wonderful, supportive team of people, inside I was angry, frustrated and jealous. I started to see other people come up in the ranks—faster than I ever had—and I was jealous. My mentor, Leanne, was also moving up and moving quickly—and instead of giving her my unconditional support (as she had always done for me), I balked. I had to be coerced into giving her my 100% support. I figured that she needed me for her success and she should be grateful for everything I did for her.

I have never been more wrong in my life. Turns out, she had already mastered the art of living with gratitude and creating a meaningful, purposeful life—and her success had little to do with me, as I soon found out. Being ungrateful and jealous caused me to make what some may think of as a rash decision—I walked away from my business. I was at the top of my game and in the top 1% in Canada. There were many reasons why I chose to do this, but one of the biggest reasons was that I felt that I was in danger of becoming toxic to my team. I was given the opportunity to start over with new business partners and I jumped over to the other side of the fence. Over the next two years, I learned some of the hardest lessons of my life.

In this new business venture, I realized two very important things. First, I had sacrificed some of my integrity by changing horses; second, that my passion for the company and products I represented had to be genuine and meaningful, and I could no longer say this. On the outside, it certainly looked like I had found success again. But what was really going on was that my husband and I were going through the most difficult time in our lives. I was married to my soul-mate and perfect life partner, and we had been living together for some time. In fact, when my husband ran into some trouble in his own career, I was the one who had supported both of us with my first business. I never imagined the opposite would happen only a year later.

Going through the experience of extreme financial stress, borderline depression and most definitely a lack of faith, I learned so much about myself. And what I found during those two years were the power of faith and gratitude in turning my life around. My daughter was born during this time, which is one of the things I am most grateful for in my life. It is because of her that I finally found faith. Faith is so important when it comes to living a successful, meaningful and purposeful life. And it was something I had struggled with for so many years. As I started to develop faith, I also began to ask for forgiveness. I forgave myself first and let go of any guilt I carried. Then I also asked some of the most important people in my life for forgiveness (some in person, some in letters that I never mailed or emails that were never sent); I also finally showed gratitude for them in my life.

It was in mending the relationship with Leanne that the door became open once again for me to return to the team and the business I had left two years prior. However, unlike before, I took my time making this decision. I had already come to the conclusion a few months earlier to walk away from the new business, but I hadn't quite figured out what I was going to do. Eventually, I realized that I was still very passionate about the products I would be representing if I went back to my first business. I was also grateful that Leanne was open to having me back, and that the company allowed me to return.

The two years that have followed have been nothing short of incredible. I finally achieved the major business goal I had been so hungry for before I quit. Through my work with daily gratitude, my ever growing faith in God and my ability to finally **be happy now**, my life did a complete 180° turn in just over eight months. I have been awarded several accolades, often alongside my teammates: now, I am cheering the loudest for them when they are rewarded! My daily gratitude practice is so ingrained now that I cannot go to sleep without completing my three daily gratitudes and when I wake up in the morning; gratitude is part of my first thoughts. I truly love my life today and am very grateful for what I have been able to create in such a short time. I look forward to sharing my experiences with the power of gratitude as we walk through the *30 Days of Gratitude* together.

My suggestion is to read each Day of Gratitude in the evening or before you go to bed and implement your new habit or take action the following day. If you need a bit of time to add a new habit or to complete your actions, take a few days to do so and then get back to the book! Some of these habits will be easy to stick to and the changes simple to make. Some of them will be much more challenging; I invite you to spend most of your time here. The more resistant you are to a suggestion or making a change, the more likely it is to have the biggest impact on your life, once you are able to make the change.

Section 1

Creating Gratitude Habits

To speak gratitude is courteous and pleasant, to enact gratitude is generous and noble, but to live gratitude is to touch Heaven.

Johannes A. Gaertner

Day 1—Starting Your Day With Gratitude

How you start your day is essentially how you live your life. Every single day presents an opportunity to start again; it is a blank slate on which you can create your life. Think of today as the only day you have: you are in the driver's seat every step of the way, from the first moment you open your eyes until the moment you go to sleep. All of the actions you took in the past brought you to this day and have influenced the person you are today.

> *Yesterday is history. Tomorrow is a mystery. Today is a gift.*
> —Eleanor Roosevelt

Be honest with yourself, are you starting your days on a positive note or a negative note? What are the first thoughts that come into your mind when you wake up and take your first few conscious breaths? For many people, their primary thought is panic—the alarm goes off and they are already thinking about the fact that they are going to be late. Instead of facing the day, they decide to press snooze and bury themselves back under the covers. When the alarm goes off again, they are now in a real panic because they are definitely late! They rush out of bed, hop into the shower, and all they can think about is how busy their day is going to be. Or worse, they pick up their smart phone and start checking email, squinting at the screen, still in a state of semi-sleep. Does this seem like a way to set yourself up for success?

On this first day of your *30 Days of Gratitude*, here are a few ideas on how to start your day:

- Make sure your phone is **turned off** and in another room before you go to sleep to resist the temptation to look at it first thing in the morning. There are very few emergency situations in life that require you to keep your phone by your side every minute of the day. If you must keep it by your bed, use the do not disturb function when sleeping.
- Use an alarm or tablet that has different sound options, so that you can have a nicer sound waking you up. This way your phone *is not immediately accessible when you awaken.*
- Before getting out of bed, take a moment to say **Thank You** for another day. This day is a gift, so take a moment to thank God, Spirit, The Universe, or whatever you choose, for another day of life.
- Once your feet hit the floor, say **Thank You** with every step you take as you walk through the hallway, to the bathroom, or into the kitchen.

After you've woken up a bit, one of the best first actions to do in the morning is to:

a) Workout
b) Check your email
c) Read an inspirational book
d) Take a shower

The best option here, and the one that is recommended by many of the most successful people in the world, is to read an inspirational book for thirty minutes first thing in the morning. You can do this while enjoying a cup of coffee or tea, or while drinking warm water with lemon. If you're not sure what I mean by inspirational book, take a look at the list I have shared in Appendix A. Many people choose to read Scripture. This helps to cement your state of mind for the day. To paraphrase Darren Hardy, publisher of *Success Magazine*, there are very few parts of the day that you can control—but what you do first thing in the morning and right before you go to sleep—are parts that you can. He calls these the **bookends** of the day. Day 1 and Day 2 of gratitude are all about the bookends.

Your Turn to Take Action, Day 1:

Choose one of the ideas for a morning ritual and start it tomorrow morning. As you become more accustomed to using these suggestions in your daily routine, you can add more changes. Trying to change too many things at once may lead to frustration or limited success.

Once you've established a morning ritual, I challenge you to set your alarm thirty minutes earlier, so that you can start to read an inspirational book before starting your day. Within about a week, your body will have adjusted to less sleep and you'll start to wake up looking forward to that period of silence every morning, with your cup of tea and your book.

Day 2—The Most Important Evening Ritual

When I say the most important evening ritual, I'm not referring to brushing your teeth, but to the habit of being grateful for three specific things before you go to bed every night.

This practice has been shared by so many successful mentors that I believe it may be the **most important** gratitude habit out there. I first learned about it when I had the opportunity to see Shawn Achor, author of *The Happiness Advantage,* speak at an event. He shared a few simple ways to turn your life around and be happy in twenty-one days. Achor suggested writing out three things you were grateful for that day before going to bed. Every day it had to be something different and specific. There are many ways you could do this, in a journal, on a tablet, even on your phone. He shared a story about a woman who documented her gratitude on her phone; if she was feeling down during the day, she'd simply flip through her list of gratitude and her mood would change.

Creating this habit can truly change your life. In the past, I had done something similar using *The Secret Gratitude Book.* Every evening I would write one page on daily gratitude, and one page of gratitude intentions in the present tense. Even though this was fairly effective, I stopped doing it because I found it to be somewhat time consuming.

In the end, I combined the two exercises—I started writing three things that I was grateful for that day and I added a fourth gratitude intention, written in the present tense. And I ended up doing it for a lot longer than twenty-one days. The impact on my life, though difficult to measure, has been nothing short of wonderful, as you will see from the examples I've shared below.

Here is an example of the exercise:

Sept 7, 2011
I am grateful for the new subscribers to my newsletter
I am grateful for my tasty sandwich for lunch
I am grateful for the DVD and book Leanne gave me today
I am grateful to be a Gold Director (next leadership level I was working towards)

Almost twelve weeks to the day of when I started my daily gratitude and intention, I became a Gold Director. To understand what this means, to achieve this level it takes four consecutive weeks of sales of approximately $10,000 USD. Completing such a business challenge takes a great team, and I am very grateful for the incredible people I attracted into my life to achieve it. In fact, I achieved my goal several months before I had intended, thanks, in part, to daily gratitude.

To continue this trend, my next gratitude intention was *I am truly grateful to be living in our own home,* as we were renting an apartment at the time. Twelve weeks later, we closed the deal on our first family home. This habit is so ingrained in my life that in a year and a half, I have missed only two nights. I am still writing every night before I go to bed, no matter how tired I am and no matter how late it is. This is especially effective after a difficult day, as it helps your mind turn to positive thoughts before heading to sleep. Not only that, you are actually creating a journal for your life! Have you ever wanted to write in a journal but never seemed to have the time? Since the daily gratitude is meant to be specific and different every night, it actually becomes a chronicle of your life and events that happen. I cannot stress this enough—if there is only one habit you learn from this book—this is the **most important**. Do not give up! Keep going beyond twenty-one days and you will see how your life can magically change.

Your Turn to Take Action, Day 2:

Immediately after putting this book down, place your tablet, phone, notepad or journal on your bedside table. Tonight, before nodding off to sleep, write three things for which you are grateful. Make it specific to that day. Add one more gratitude intention for a goal that you would like to achieve, and write it in the present tense. This should be the very last thing you do before your turn off the light.

Day 3 —The Power of Our Words

The importance of living from gratitude daily has been shared by many teachers and mentors throughout the ages. Why this more than anything else? First, it is something that is very simple to do, yet most people do not take the time to do it. Perhaps it is because we have grown up in a culture where it is much easier to complain and to wish for what we don't have; "I wish it wasn't raining today" or "I am tired of this old car, I wish I had a new one". It seems so much easier to fall into this pattern than to change the pattern and focus on being more grateful.

What can we do to start thinking from a place of gratitude, rather than a place of lack or scarcity? Let's start with something that we can control: the power of our words. Our words carry a lot of weight, and it's important to take great care in the words that we think—let alone the words that we speak or write. That's why it's important to always take a moment and think before you speak, text or write an email. I love the way that Robin Sharma puts it: "Use the language of leadership vs. the phrases of victims."

Here is an example of what that would look like:

This is a tough time of year. People don't have any money to buy things. I haven't had any luck closing any sales. I'm tired of getting no, after no, after no. The problem is that our products are too expensive!

Here is another way to say this using the *language of leadership*:

This time of year is great for making sales; people always find money to buy things that improve their health and their lifestyle. Every person I connect with, even if they say no, brings me one step closer to connecting with the right person. I am putting more energy into creating success this week! I am so grateful for all of the sales that are coming my way!

Have you ever felt someone's emotions just from opening their email message? You can literally feel despair, pain or anger from the energy of the message. I suggest waiting before checking your email in the morning, to avoid starting the day with this kind of negative energy, should your inbox contain one or more of these kinds of messages. Our words are so very powerful: it's up to us to choose whether we allow them to have a positive or negative influence on our everyday lives and on the lives of others.

The first step in understanding the power of words is to notice and become aware of our own self-talk. Take a moment to listen to your own self-talk. Not sure what I mean by this? Take a look in the mirror and listen to what you are saying to yourself. Are you treating yourself with love and gratitude or with negativity and cruelty? Next, take a look at how you are interacting with other people. Are you choosing your words before speaking? Do people get upset when they receive an email from you? Or are they simply afraid to answer the phone when you call? By becoming aware of your current state, be it positive or negative, this will help you to make changes and to apply the lessons you are learning throughout this book.

Your Turn to Take Action, Day 3:

Take a small spiral notebook around with you for the day. Using a plus or minus sign, keep track of the way in which you are speaking, not only to other people, but also to yourself. Becoming aware of whether you tip the scales positively or negatively will help you shift to a more positive outlook, and help you understand how to bring more gratitude into your life.

Day 4—Stop the Negative!

One of the reasons it can be difficult to live with an attitude of gratitude is due to all of the negative influences that we are bombarded with every day. Take a look at the list below and check off the ones you watch or read on a daily basis.

Negative Influences List:

- ☐ Morning newspaper(s)
- ☐ News periodical(s) (TIME, Maclean's, The Economist, The New Yorker)
- ☐ News channel on TV (CNN, City News, CTV News)
- ☐ News radio at home or in the car on the way to work
- ☐ Fiction novels with themes of war, destruction, murder etc.
- ☐ Television shows that focus on crime, drama or the supernatural
- ☐ News apps or email/twitter alerts from news channels
- ☐ Reality television
- ☐ Evening news during dinner or before bed

It's no wonder it's such a challenge to stay optimistic when we are surrounded with so much negativity—both real and imaginary. Take a look at your results from the exercise in Day 3. If your results tend to fall into the negative category, chances are you checked off at least three to five of the items above.

The following analogy by Earl Nightingale, in *The Strangest Secret*, demonstrates why it is so important to know what seeds we are planting in our minds:

Suppose a farmer has some land and it's good, fertile land. Now, the land gives the farmer a choice. He may plant in that land whatever he chooses. The land doesn't care. It's up to the farmer to make the decision.

Now let's say that the farmer has two seeds in his hand—one a seed of corn; the other is nightshade, a deadly poison. He digs two little holes in the earth and he plants both seeds; one corn, the other nightshade. He covers up the holes, waters, and takes care of the land.

What will happen? Invariably, the land will return what's planted. Remember, the land doesn't care. It will return poison in just as wonderful abundance as it will corn. So up come the two plants—one corn, one poison.

In order for you to cultivate success and wealth in your life, you've got to change the seeds that you are planting. The more negative influences you see and read during the day, the more challenging it becomes to plant positive seeds. To be able to live a life of gratitude, the seeds of your mind must be sown from a place of gratitude and love, not fear or lack.

Your Turn to Take Action, Day 4:

Starting today and for the next seven days, reduce or remove one of the items you checked off from the negatives influences list. The next chapter will offer ideas on how to replace constructive things for those with negative impact and, like the farmer, allow you to plant more positive seeds.

Day 5—Feed Your Mind

What can we do to make it easier to feed our minds with more positive influences? Starting with the list from Day 4, I will offer some alternatives.

- **Morning newspaper(s)**—How much time to do you spend reading the paper in the morning? For many years I used to read the daily paper; I was single and it was nice to have something to read while eating breakfast. After some time I realized that starting my day with stories of deception, murder, crime, financial crises, potential terrorist attacks and even negative movie reviews was not the best way to start my day. Although I am now married and have a busy life with my daughter, I still like to start my day with a bit of reading. However, I choose books with a positive or uplifting theme (mostly non-fiction) that put me in a great state of mind for the day. Currently, I am working my way through Dr. Wayne Dyer's *Change Your Thoughts, Change Your Life—Living the Wisdom of the Tao*. I recommend this as a great choice for morning reading, since the chapters are short and you can take the day to digest the content.

- **News periodical(s) (TIME, Maclean's, The Economist, The New Yorker)**—If you love to read magazines, there are many other options besides news periodicals. You may argue that some of this reading is essential for the type of work you do or business you are in; certainly, there are some sectors that require you to have specific and up-to-the-minute knowledge, but do you need to read more than one magazine? Why not choose the one you cannot live without? Or substitute with a subscription to *Success Magazine*—my absolute favorite magazine—full of great business ideas, positive messages, successful role models and a free audio CD every month. If you have a habit of picking up celebrity magazines or other types of fashion or style magazines, ask yourself if you feel better or worse after reading them.

- **News channel on TV (CNN, City News, CTV News)**—I have yet to find a good reason why these news channels are on all day long—especially since there is a lack of good news shared. If you have a really good reason why the same, often depressing news needs to run on a loop throughout the day, please share it on our Facebook page: https://www.facebook.com/30daysofgratitudebook. I see these news feeds in medical and dental offices, in airports, many coffee shops and even in grocery stores. The majority of the time the news has **zero** impact on your life. The other one percent of the time, someone will text, email or call you when it does. Turn it off! Play classical music instead or display a virtual fish tank or fireplace. These options are much more relaxing and allow you to think more clearly.

- **News radio at home or in the car on the way to work**—You're probably thinking, *but I need to hear the traffic report*, or *I have to know what the weather is like*. If that's the case, listen to the traffic report **once** and turn it off. For the weather, a simple weather app does the trick: check it before you leave the house so that you know

15

how to dress for the day. Two things we definitely cannot control—the traffic and the weather. An alternative solution to the radio? Make your car your university on wheels! There are so many books available in audio format, and many can be borrowed for free from your local library. As I mentioned earlier, if you subscribe to *Success Magazine*, you'll receive a free CD every month. I have over four years of CDs from *Success Magazine* in my car. In addition, I really enjoy John C. Maxwell's audio version of his books on leadership, as he reads them himself in his beautiful baritone voice. Imagine you spent two hours a day commuting—that's ten hours a week of learning and 500 hours a year! Your life would be very different if you made this change.

- **Fiction novels with themes of war, destruction, murder, etc.**—If you find that you need fiction books as an escape from your life, it's probably time to take a look at the life you are living. What is it that you need to escape from? For others, fiction can be a healthy break from your daily life and if you're like me, a welcome change from non-fiction reading (one of my favorite reads is *The Dresden Files*, a fantasy series—although not before bed, as magical, evil creatures will fill my dreams!). As Jim Rohn says, *"Successful people have libraries, the rest have big screen tvs."* What are you filling your library with? There are thousands of books on personal development, self-esteem, creating wealth, being happy, and thousands more biographies of successful people in every field. These are all great ways to fill your personal library if your goals include building your self-esteem, living from a place of gratitude, and continual personal development.

- **Television shows that focus on crime, drama or the supernatural**—Similar to the point above, if you're choosing to live in someone else's fictional world instead of or as an escape from your own, then you are not living your life to the fullest. Furthermore, if you are watching these kinds of things before bed, what are you feeding your subconscious before you go to sleep? I personally loved watching CSI, usually about an hour before bed, but since I quite that habit several years ago; I sleep much better and have fewer nightmares.

- **News apps or email/twitter alerts from news channels**—See point above about news channels on TV. Stop the alerts. Today.

- **Reality television**—Best said by Denis Waitley, *"Prime time is that period between 6 and 10 p.m. during which most of the general public watches television. Commercials in prime time are the most expensive, approaching a million dollars per minute. Your real success in life will take a quantum leap when you stop watching other people making money in their professions performing in prime time, and start living your own dreams and goals in prime time."*

- **Evening news during dinner or before bed**—This is very important to avoid, especially right before bed. Day 7 will provide some great insights on the importance of evening rituals.

Your Turn to Take Action, Day 5:

Turn it off. The TV news channel, the radio, the Twitter alerts. Anything that is news related or doesn't make you feel **great** after watching or reading it—turn it off. If you consider yourself addicted to television, that's ok, start by reducing the amount of television you are watching by one hour a night in the first week, and reduce it by more as the month continues. Using the suggestions above chose something constructive to do in its place, or else you may turn the TV back on to avoid boredom. This is not something that will be done in one day; it will take a little bit of work to achieve. And when you have found the right balance, you will be grateful to have taken the steps to change it!

Day 6—Fuel Your Body

Now that we've taken care of the mind, let's look at the rest of the body. Did you know that gratitude can be a very important part of being healthy and achieving optimal health? How many of you know someone who hates their body or a part of their body? Or maybe you've felt this way about your own body at some point? The challenge is that if we are giving our body negative energy and thoughts, then it becomes very difficult to achieve our physical goals. Our body is made up of 70-80% water. Water is very responsive to words and thoughts. The book by Dr. Masaru Emoto, *Hidden Messages in Water*, shows how water crystals are affected by words and thoughts. In short, his work shows us that: *Negative, hateful messages = ugly crystals. Beautiful, positive messages = beautiful crystals*. His research was shared in the movie *What the Bleep Do We Know!?*. The most important message that I learned from his work is that our bodies are very responsive to our thoughts.

A great place to start if you are looking to release weight is to be grateful for your body as it is right now. When you look in the mirror, allow yourself to compliment the parts of your body that you do like. Do you have beautiful eyes? Perhaps you often get compliments on your hair, your smile or another body part. Why not give yourself the same compliment? This is not the same as being self-centered or narcissistic; this is about loving your body and being grateful for it. The more you are able to love your body as it is right now, the easier it is to release weight. And get rid of the scale! Do not allow yourself to be a slave to the numbers. My simple recommendations are, first, pay attention to how your clothes fit—are they getting looser or tighter? And second, know your waist size: healthy is below 35" for women and below 40" for men. Those are the only numbers you have to worry about, not what the scale says. Ask yourself this, if the number goes up on the scale, do you feel happy or sad? The truth is, the scale has absolutely nothing to do with your happiness! Remember that next time you walk by a scale at the gym.

How do you react when someone gives you a compliment? Do you cringe, make an excuse, and explain why you look great that day or why your eyes are so blue? Learning to be grateful for a compliment and simply saying **thank you** can be very difficult for many people. If you can learn to accept compliments, it can make a huge difference in how you feel about your body over time. Often we are very harsh critics of our own bodies and learning to accept a compliment is all about seeing your beauty through someone else's eyes.

Another way to use gratitude to help you achieve optimal health is to slow down and give thanks before you eat. If you take the time to eat at the table with your family whenever possible (instead of in front of the TV or computer), and pause before you eat, this helps you to become more aware of what you are putting into your month. Being grateful for your food is also important, as we often take for granted that we have easy access to an endless supply of food. Taking the time to chew your food, and drinking water at the end of your meal helps with digestion as well. These few changes alone may have a positive effect on your waistline.

Lastly, eating real, whole food that comes from the earth or as close to nature as possible is most important. As Michael Polland, author of *In Defense of Food: An Eater's Manifesto,* says *"Eat food. Not too much. Mostly plants."*

It's a simple model to live by. Whole foods and filtered water keep your cells happy, and happy cells make you happy!

Your Turn to Take Action, Day 6:

Learn to accept a compliment. Say thank you and resist the urge to comment or return the compliment. Eat at least one meal a day, for one week, at the table with your spouse, partner, kids, parents or roommates. If you live alone, that's ok, enjoy a quiet moment while eating a meal at the table in silence, and focus on the taste and textures of the food. Take a moment before you eat to say grace or simply be thankful for the food that is on your plate.

And finally, take a look in the mirror tonight and give yourself a sincere compliment. Not sure what to say? Look into your own eyes and say "I love you". Yes, it will be uncomfortable at first. Do it for ten days straight and your self-image will start to change for the better.

Day 7—More Evening Rituals

As I shared in Day 2, the most important thing you can do before you go to sleep is your three daily gratitudes. In this chapter, I'll share a few other suggestions to help you prepare your mind for sleep, by helping your brain focus on the positive aspects of life before your subconscious takes over.

The hour prior to sleep is the most important in determining the quality of your sleep. And what does this have to do with gratitude? If you are practicing the habit of three daily gratitudes before you go to sleep, it's important to look at what your state of mind is before you do this exercise. As I shared before, our words are very powerful and contain energy, and by having a positive state of mind before completing your gratitude exercise this allows your gratitude intention to come true even more quickly. Not only that, a restful, rejuvenating six to eight hours of sleep can increase your chances of success. Let's take a look at your last hour before sleep.

First, the most important things to avoid:

- Exercise—I love to exercise, but exercise is best done at least two hours before bed. This allows your body to have a proper cool down, allows for endorphin levels to return back to normal, and allows you to refuel your body without going to bed with a full stomach.
- Television—One of my golden rules is no television in the bedroom. In fact, when my husband and I first started dating, I made it clear that this would never happen (in case it was a deal breaker!). There are many reasons why

this is so important, not only because of the content on television, but also because the light that is emitted from televisions and other screens does not allow your brain to rest. If you must have a television or screen in your bedroom (or your children's bedrooms) make sure they are turned off (complete power off, not sleep mode) and covered for sleep.

- The news of any kind—Whether it's the 11 o'clock news, a newspaper or a news periodical, the news should most importantly be avoided before bed. If not, the news will feed your subconscious as you sleep.

- Technology—Turn off your laptop, phone, tablet or computer at least thirty minutes before bed. Yes, I did say turn off your phone. There are very few professions that require your phone to be on all night. And if you are worried about an emergency with family, you can set-up your phone on silent (allow phone calls only) or do not disturb with a setting that allows specific numbers to ring (i.e. your children or parents). These functions are easily accessible on most smart phones by looking at the settings for your ring tones and also engaging the do not disturb function.

Now let's look at some suggestions on what to do before going to bed. First, why not try reading? As I mentioned, there are thousands of incredible books on personal development, leadership, mentoring and healthy lifestyle. Visit your local library, in person or online (you can get books online for eReaders and audiobooks as well) and start to read a few. I have included a list of my favorites in Appendix A. "Old-fashioned" reading with a real book is often a nice change from technology, but if you choose to read on an eReader or tablet, make sure you're not checking email and Facebook at the same time.

A warm bath or shower is also a great idea to help you unwind. Interestingly, after a warm bath your body temperature may rise a bit, which can help you to fall asleep. When relaxing in the tub or shower, do your best to be present in that moment. See if you can quiet your mind and simply enjoy the water. Take the time to relax every muscle in your body. And lock the door! This is your time to let go of the tension from the day and to allow yourself to be in a relaxed, positive mindset in preparation for your daily gratitude ritual.

A few other suggestions would be to do some quiet meditation or prayer. If you've never meditated before, there are many resources to help you with this, including guided meditation audio programs. My suggestion is to start with five minutes, in a position that is comfortable for you: sitting in a chair, a cushion on the floor, leaning on a wall, or lying down. Make sure the environment around you is quiet. And simply try to focus on your breath. That's it, just pay attention to breathing in and out, filling your lungs with life-giving air. Sometimes focusing on one simple thing will help to quiet that chattering voice in your head that we all hear most of the time. If prayer is important for you, this would also be an excellent time of day for prayer. And in the last five minutes before you turn off the lights, complete your daily gratitudes.

Your Turn to Take Action, Day 7:

The last hour before you go to sleep is very important, so turn off the electronics and find some quiet time for you! Turn off your phone. Yes, you can do it and everything will be ok. Choose one suggestion that feels most comfortable for you and try it for a week. If you like it, stick with it; if not, try a different one. And once you're in a positive, grateful state, complete your three daily gratitudes and your gratitude intention. Sweet dreams!

Day 8—How to be Happy Now

*Happiness depends more on how life strikes you than
on what happens.*—Andy Rooney

As we start the second week of this program (or perhaps longer
if you've been taking the time to implement some of the new
habits), you are probably noticing some positive changes in your
life. It's also possible that you aren't seeing any real changes yet,
and you may be wondering why. If you're doing the action steps
and making the changes, but not seeing any positive outcomes,
don't get discouraged. Keep at it, and continue with your daily
gratitude and working on your positive attitude. Each person
has their own path, and yours may be a little bit longer. You
will see results if you believe in yourself and have faith that this
does work!

It's also possible that there may be an underlying reason for the
lack of positive changes. Perhaps deep down you aren't truly
happy right now. Our emotions tend to drive our thoughts and
our thoughts lead to our actions, and the outcomes that make
up our lives. If our emotions are not in line with our thoughts,
then our actions (and therefore the circumstances we create) will
not give us our desired results. Another way to look at this is to
think back to the example of planting seeds in the mind. If your
underlying emotional state is negative, and you have feelings of
anger, resentment, disappointment, depression or guilt, then the
seeds you are planting are negative or poisonous. Therefore, even if
you've been following the program diligently, the thoughts created
from these seeds will have a drop of "poison" in them. And the
actions (outcomes) that are created will not be what you desire.

The key is to build your foundation of emotions on the positive side of things—feelings of love, gratitude, joy, faith and passion. How can you do that if life is challenging for you right now? Again, the power of gratitude can help you with being happy now. Here is a quick solution to change your underlying emotions to gratitude: every time you feel one of the negative emotions, remind yourself of something for which to be grateful. This well-known proverb reminds us that we can always find something to be grateful for:

> *I cried because I had no shoes on my feet, until I met the man who had no feet.*

There are so many simple things to be grateful for:

- I am grateful for my eyes to see.
- I am grateful to be able to walk or move without assistance.
- I am grateful for my independence.
- I am grateful for the food on my table (as much or as little as it may be—close to 900 million people worldwide do not have enough to eat).
- I am grateful for the clothing on my back (as new or as old as it may be).
- I am grateful to have a roof over my head.
- I am grateful to be able to read.

Another key thing is to allow yourself to feel the negative emotion, and then let it pass through you. The important message here is not to avoid negative emotions, but to allow them to pass without staying blocked inside of you. Once you have let the harmful emotion pass through, use your simple gratitudes to help you quickly shift to a positive emotion. When successful people experience negative emotions or bad feelings, they allow them to pass through quickly and move on. This is what distinguishes the most successful people from others who struggle to thrive. Using this strategy may help you to do the same.

Your Turn to Take Action, Day 8:

Create your own list of simple things for which to be grateful and keep it in your wallet, back pocket or purse. Pull it out whenever you need a quick emotional shift. You can start your list here and copy it on to a card, or even make a note in your phone.

I am grateful for:

1. _____
2. _____
3. _____
4. _____
5. _____

Day 9—How Gratitude Helps with Grief

There are times in our lives when the strategies shared in the last chapter aren't enough to change how we feel. We all go through difficult times in our lives, and sometimes we are faced with what we would call a tragedy. Losing someone you love, being diagnosed with an illness or degenerative disease, going through a major accident or disaster, experiencing a divorce, separation, or the loss of a child—any one of these can easily bring on sad and negative emotions. It can often be very difficult to get out of the darkness.

How can gratitude be a part of the process? How is it possible to find the good when life seems to have taken a turn for the worse? I recently experienced what would be considered a life tragedy. I was pregnant with my second child, and had passed the "safe" first trimester when I miscarried at fifteen weeks. The event itself was very difficult for me; it was both physically and mentally traumatic. And the aftermath, after having shared the joyful news with so many people, could have been even more challenging. Yet that night, even though we had lost our child, I found a way to be grateful:

> *I am truly grateful that my daughter was at daycare today*
> *I am truly grateful that the police were able to break down the door* (I was home alone and the front door was locked, so this had to be done for EMS to enter)
> *I am truly grateful that my husband and best friend were at the hospital with me*

It may seem strange, even perverse, to continue with my daily gratitude practice after such a difficult day. Here is what I know to be true (for me):

The situation was truly out of my control. Our child's spirit had already returned to be with God and my body did what it had to do, as nature intended.

Nothing I did caused the situation or could have changed the outcome.

Life will continue to move on, regardless of what happened.

I have the choice to move on with it, or remain in the darkness of the day.

So I chose to move on. I chose to continue with my gratitude practice and to honour my faith. I connected with the people I care about and took extra time to be grateful for the wonderful people who surround me. I spent more time with my beautiful daughter and felt more grateful than ever for her perfection.

In the days that followed, I continued to be even more grateful than I had been before this happened. And you know what? Every cloud, no matter how dark, does have a silver lining. In this case, I was even more driven to write this book and share my experiences with you. I am more grateful for the one child I do have. I am excited and grateful for our plans for the upcoming summer. And I am grateful for all of the love and kindness given to me by the incredible people in my life, during this most difficult time.

Your Turn to Take Action, Day 9:

If you have been touched by a tragedy recently, or perhaps you are still holding on to pain from something that happened long ago, why not try to find gratitude in that situation? See if you can reframe what happened and find the good. Or even see what good may have occurred since that time. And if you find that truly nothing seems to help, I suggest you connect with a trusted professional and work through your grief together. And use this book and some of the daily actions to support you as you work through your journey out of the darkness.

Day 10—Affirmations of Gratitude

Only good lies before me.—Louise Hay

Finally, the chapter on affirmations! How many of you grew up watching *Saturday Night Live* and remember Stuart Smalley? He was my first introduction to affirmations: *"I'm good enough, I'm smart enough, and doggone it, people like me!"* Of course this was a spoof on affirmations, but as I started to study different authors, such as Louise Hay, Dr. Wayne Dyer and Cheryl Richardson, I learned more about affirmations and the power they possess.

Let's be honest for a moment—we all have that little voice in our heads that is constantly speaking to us. Even as I write this book my little voice is offering its opinion: *should I talk about Stuart Smalley; am I sharing too much or too little; does the book make sense to people?* It can be very hard to turn it off! Perhaps you're nodding in agreement and wondering if you can ever have some peace and quiet already. What I really love about affirmations is that they allow you to quiet that voice, even for just a moment, and focus on what is important. I have been using different affirmations for some time and I find them extremely useful. In my opinion, Louise Hay is the queen of affirmations. Her most famous book, *You Can Heal Your Life*, is filled with incredible affirmations that can truly make a difference in your life. If you haven't already read this book, I highly recommend adding it to your list.

Here is how I personally use affirmations of gratitude in my life. I have already shared that when I first wake up in the morning, I say *Thank you* as I walk to the bathroom. I like to thank my bed for a great sleep (most of the time) and I also say *I am grateful for another day on this earth.* I remind myself that not everyone woke up this morning, and that not everyone was able to get up and walk out of bed.

Throughout the day, I will say and think of affirmations in my head, or say them out loud, depending on who is around and how I feel. Below are a few examples that I use:

- I am grateful for my beautiful daughter and my amazing husband (especially useful if we've had an argument).
- Thank you (as I walk up and down the stairs, which is not something to be taken for granted).
- Thank you for this food, Amen (before eating).
- I am grateful for my amazing week (especially when I have come across a challenge).

Moreover, when I am walking outside or even around the house, I often carry thoughts of gratitude for different people in my life. It is actually fairly easy to use affirmations of gratitude throughout your day. And why is it important? For one thing, it's easier to stay positive when your mind chatter is quiet and you are focussing on being grateful. So why not give it a try?

Your Turn to Take Action, Day 10:

Pick a couple of moments during the day to use a simple affirmation of gratitude. For example, take a moment to thank the mail carrier who delivered your mail. Or how about saying thank you that your car brought you safely to your destination? You could also thank other drivers on the road for driving safely. There are many moments during the day to express gratitude. For a full lesson on this, read *You Can Create an Exceptional Life*, an outstanding book by Louise Hay and Cheryl Richardson.

Day 11—Giving Thanks

One my favorite ways to show gratitude is through simple gestures of thanks to the people I care about. There are many ways to do this and I'll share a few that I have done myself.

Thank-You Cards

I love buying cards! Yes, real, physical cards that I have to mail. I buy them in bulk and always have a varied collection on hand. There are many ways to use Thank-You cards to express gratitude and encouragement.

- Send a Thank-You card to someone who gave you great service (within 24 hours if possible)—it could be your mechanic, massage therapist, hairdresser, cleaning service, lawn care, contractor, dentist; the possibilities are endless. Receiving a card for impressive service is often seen as a gift by those who get them, since it can be rare to receive this type of gratitude from a client. Many people are proud to be recognized, and will post the card for all to see.
- Start a 30 Days of Thank-You Cards challenge. Every day for 30 days, send a Thank-You card to someone in your life. It could be family, friends, service providers, a long lost contact, or even someone you just met. This is a truly enjoyable exercise, and I always end up looking forward to who I can thank next! Plan ahead and purchase a stack of cards and stamps, and print return address labels to make the task easier. Make a list of people to thank; this way, you can avoid duplicates and make sure you don't leave

anyone out. This is an easy way to turn your life around, particularly if you've been in a rut or lack motivation. You can also make this part of your daily exercise routine if you choose to walk to the mailbox daily.

- If thirty days is too big of a task for you, start with sending out one or two Thank-You cards a week, for ten weeks. This will have a similar effect as the 30 Days challenge.
- Send physical cards to congratulate team members or employees for their accomplishments and service.
- It's also important to send cards to express sympathy and support when needed.

In a world where everything is instant through email, texting and social media, receiving a card in the mail is very special. The person who sent it to you took the time to think of you and to say thank you.

However, I still believe there are ways to use social media to express gratitude. For example, there are many notable things we can do with Facebook. One of my favourites was the month of gratitude; every day I posted a status update about someone for whom I was grateful, tagging them when possible. This was a straightforward activity (and did not involve stamps or cards), and I enjoyed the daily ritual of sharing why I was grateful for different people in my life. Occasionally, I would thank a small group of people that were in my life, such as my mommy group, which allowed me to include as many people as possible in thirty days. When I posted that I was grateful for my husband on Facebook, everyone thought it was our anniversary! People suggested he buy me flowers, regardless of the fact that our anniversary was several months earlier.

The differences between this challenge and the Thank-You cards, is that the Facebook gratitude challenge is public and short-lived, while a Thank-You card is private and can last for months or even years. I have kept several meaningful cards, and even post some of them on my bulletin board or put them on my desk, as a reminder of the special moment I received them.

Your Turn to Take Action, Day 11:

Choose one of the activities outlined above and implement it within the next week. It doesn't matter which one you choose; even if it's buying cards to have them ready to send when you receive great service, that's a good start. If you already have a supply of cards, take one out and write it to someone you are grateful for, right now. Mail it within 24 hours. This simple gesture will bring a smile to your face and will definitely bring a smile to theirs.

Now that we are over a third of the way through the *30 Days of Gratitude*, I invite you to look back on the past eleven days or so, and ask yourself if anything has changed. Have you begun to implement some of the habits? Do you find that you are thinking about more ways to be grateful every day? I would like to invite you to join our community on Facebook, where people can share how this program has affected their lives, and share ideas on how gratitude can become a daily habit.

https://www.facebook.com/30daysofgratitudebook

The next section of the book will cover more about how gratitude is important when creating a vision to help make your goals and dreams come true. You'll be given a step-by-step plan on how to plan your year, with a specific focus on the next ninety days. I'll also share why it's important to have a few mentors in your life, and the value of surrounding yourself with incredible people.

Section 2

Gratitude and Designing Your Life

*Gratitude makes sense of our past, brings peace for today,
and creates a vision for tomorrow.*

Melody Beattie

Day 12—Create Your Vision

As we move into the second section of this book, we will start to look at how gratitude plays an important part in creating our lives. And yes, we do all play a part. As Dr. Wayne Dyer puts it,

> *The more you see yourself as what you'd like to become, and act as if what you want is already there, the more you'll activate those dormant forces that will collaborate to transform your dream into your reality.*

A vision statement is a chance for you to create your future on paper and then do the work and walk out the steps to make that vision a reality. If you have never done this exercise before it can be a little bit daunting but also a lot of fun! A vision statement may also be the fuel to create a vision board; a visual representation using pictures and words to map out where you are going. The next chapter will give you details on how to build a vision board.

Here are a few tips to help you create an incredible five year vision:

- Find a quiet place where you won't be disturbed for at least twenty minutes. Lock the bathroom door if you have to! A quiet place outside is best if the weather allows.
- Bring a notepad or tablet to write with. First close your eyes and begin to imagine what your life could be like in five years, if money, time or health were no longer holding you back. Let go of any preconceived notions

about your job or business, or any kind of expectations you may feel are forced upon you. Imagine what a day in your life could be like. Where do you wake up? Who do you wake up next to? What does the room look like? What do you see when you look out the window? Are there kids or pets nearby? What does your morning look like? How about lunch time? Who do you spend your afternoon with? Does everyone eat dinner together or are you attending different activities and events? What do you do before you go to sleep?

- Now in the **present tense**, write out what your ideal day looks like five years from now. Choose a date that resonates with you. You can also reflect on accomplishments you had along the way that allowed you to get to where you are at that moment in time. Write about all areas of your life including business or work, family, health & fitness, lifestyle, spirituality and personal growth. Be sure to include gratitude as you write out your vision as this truly helps to cement the images into your brain. Being grateful for what is going to happen makes it arrive much faster and with ease. If you believe that time is not linear, you know that your future already exists only it's on a different plane, so it makes sense to already be grateful for it!

- Have fun with this! The only limit to your vision is your imagination. Anything is possible! Your world can be completely different in the next five years, if you choose to create it.

To help you get started:

It is the early morning on April 18, 2018 and I am so happy and grateful to be waking up beside my beloved partner, as the morning sunshine peeks through the blinds in the window of our dream home on the water.

Take a much time and space as you need. The more details in your vision, the more likely it is to become a reality. A vision is something very personal and I encourage you to share it with the people you love and care about. And if you feel emotional or begin to cry when you share your vision, then you know you are on the right track.

We all have two choices:
We can make a living or we can design a life.—Jim Rohn

Here is a really fun idea for sharing your vision. Have a *Come As You Are in 2018* (or five years from when you are reading this) and invite eight to twelve friends to join you, in character, as the person they have become in five years. Everyone brings a copy of their vision and either reads it out loud, or simply acts as though these things have already happened. Bring photos (use Photoshop!) of things you have accomplished, the home where you live now and your lifestyle, including trips you've taken and experiences you've had. I did this with a few friends back in 2007. We had a great time and I took the time to write out in detail how I envisioned the different parts of my life. When 2012 rolled around, I found the document again, and although I may not have accomplished everything in the vision, I did find and marry the man of my dreams, have a daughter with him, move into our dream home (for now) and accomplish many of the business and income goals I had set out. Since that time I have also re-written and updated my vision at least once a year and I found it interesting to see how my dreams had changed and expanded over the years. Rather than feeling disappointed that I haven't accomplished all of my goals, I am grateful for where I am today. Letting go of any attachments to the outcomes is what allows your vision to be realized. It's about letting go and letting God. And having faith that you will do, have and become everything you have ever wanted.

Your Turn to Take Action, Day 12:

Pause for a moment on this day and this exercise and take the time to do it. In order to effectively complete the next few exercises in the book, you'll need to have a solid foundation and your vision will provide you with that.

Day 13—Make a Vision Board

A vision board is a great tool to allow your five year vision to be realized even more quickly. I have created at least half a dozen vision boards over the past several years. Many of the things I have put on my vision boards have come true, so it's important to change and update them at least once a year. Our mind thinks in pictures and by giving it something to look at it helps to make it a reality in our physical world.

Here are a few tips to help you build your vision board:

Preparation:

- Buy magazines that you don't normally purchase—for example The Robb Report (luxury cars, homes etc.), Architectural Digest, Conde Nast Traveller.
- Save old calendars—many have great quotes and photos (or buy them in February at 75% off).
- Use Google images for specific photos that you haven't found in a magazine.
- Think BIG and allow yourself dream your impossible dreams! This is what can be really fun about the vision board.
- Choose quotes and words that inspire you. "Rev it up!" is one of my favorites. Words such as: Focus, Power, Inspiration, Leadership, Fun and Love are also effective.
- Instead of using a bristol board, you can purchase a thicker foam board from most craft stores for about $5. If you are looking for a more permanent board, purchase a frame

for a heavier cardboard and frame it. Replace the inside of the frame with a new vision board yearly.

- Before you start, cut out all of the photos, quotes and items that you'd like to have on your vision board. Make sure that you choose carefully—only put things you really, truly desire on your board. You can also use coloured paper or cardboard to accent different parts of the vision board.

Making your vision board:

- Find a large, flat surface to lay your board on.
- Arrange the photos in a collage fashion on your board. You can do this any way you like but for my most recent board, I put together the photos and quotes based on the Feng Shui bagua. I also included colour swatches from each of the bagua quadrants. Google *Feng Shui bagua* if you're interested in finding out more about how it works and for a full colour image of the bagua.
- Use an acid free glue and test it ahead of time, not all glues dry nicely.
- Place all of the photos and quotes on the board before you begin gluing.
- Add your positive emotions to the images and words before you glue them on to the board, to ensure your own positive energy is a part of your vision board.
- Be grateful for the incredible life you are creating!

A few final notes:

- Playing uplifting music or *The Secret* movie in the background can be helpful.

- A short guided meditation beforehand may also put you in the right frame of mind.
- Your vision board should make you smile when you look at it and create feelings of excitement and joy!
- Hang your vision board in a place where you will see it several times throughout your day. And take a moment to stop and look at it when you walk by.

Your Turn to Take Action, Day 13:

Make your own vision board. Or better yet, organize a vision board party! Invite a few friends over to create together. You can either prepare your photos ahead of time, or bring magazines and brochures that you can share. Put it all together, take a photo and share it on our Facebook page. My own personal vision board has been shared as well.

Day 14—Find Your Life's Purpose

Now that you know where you are going, let's look at the underlying reasons why you want to get there. What motivates you to get up every morning to do what needs to be done in order to achieve your vision? What is your purpose in life? Why were you, the very unique one-in-a-billion you, placed here on this planet? This is a deep question that many people may not have yet considered. In order to achieve greatness in this lifetime, we must understand why we are here. Each of us has a purpose to fulfill and the sooner we figure this out, the sooner we can create amazing things! Let us not leave this world without having sung our song or played our tune.

How do we do this? Here are few ideas to help you formulate your **purpose statement**. Understand that this is a work in progress and you may not find the answers just by doing this exercise. Start here and see what happens.

1. What do you enjoy most about your current job or work? Share as many things as possible.
2. When spending time with family, what do you find to be the most enjoyable?
3. Think back to a time when you were doing an activity and it felt like time was standing still; when you were truly in the moment and completely present. What were you doing? What other activities put you into this state of flow?
4. When you think about your current life situation, is there anything that you really want to change so much

that you think about it every day? What would be the opposite of this?

5. When you watch a video or read a book, what kinds of things put a smile on your face?

6. In what ways do you give to others? What services can you provide? Do these actions make you feel good?

7. What are you passionate about? Is there a cause that stirs your heart?

8. What are your values? What would you take a stand for? What types of behaviours make you angry? And what are their opposites?

From your responses, work on formulating a one to three sentence **purpose statement**. This has to be powerful enough to get you out of bed in the morning and to allow you to make choices that will move you closer to achieving your vision, not further. Without a purpose, it will be easier to stay within your comfort zone and avoid taking steps towards achieving your vision and goals. The daily gratitude practices you have learned in the first section will help you to stay in a positive state of mind as you fulfill your life's purpose day by day.

My purpose is to help thousands of men and women around the world to achieve a healthy, balanced lifestyle and the freedom to live out their life-long dreams, through personal mentorship, inspiration, leadership and with the upmost integrity.—Julie Boyer

Your Turn to Take Action, Day 14:

This is not an easy task. Perhaps you already have a **purpose statement** for yourself and if that is the case, I encourage you to take a look at it and make sure it still resonates with you. If you haven't already done this, take some time to work on it. Keep a notebook handy and write down things that make you happy or moments when you feel like you're in the flow of life and everything just seems easy. This will help you to distill your true purpose. If you find that you are stuck on this exercise, that's ok, it will come with time. Take a look at the books in Appendix A and choose a new one. Many of these books will help to inspire you and guide you to find your life's purpose.

Day 15—Review of the Past 12 Months

For most people, Jan 1st is when they take the time to create goals for the upcoming year. And for many, by the time mid-January rolls around they have already abandoned their goals for the year. Does this sound familiar? Or maybe instead of goals you call them New Year's Resolutions? I'd like to share my method of planning yearly goals that can be done at any time of the year (right now!) and reviewed or refreshed at the end of the calendar year.

How does gratitude fit into the picture when it comes to goal setting? First, it's important to keep your vision close by and make sure that your purpose is clear. It's no use setting goals that don't match your purpose or that won't bring you any closer to realizing your vision. If this is your first time setting goals, I suggest you start with a review of the past twelve months. You can write in this book or create a similar chart or spreadsheet (an extra copy can be found in Appendix D). Visit 30daysofgratitudebook.com for a downloadable PDF. This review can be done at any time, the important thing is to review your successes and be grateful for them. The categories can be changed to suit your needs; these are the ones that I have found work best for me.

Category	3 Successes	3 Areas for Improvement
Business or work		
Family		
Health & Fitness		
Lifestyle		
Spirituality		
Education & Personal Growth		

The three areas for improvement will serve as a guide when preparing your goals for the next twelve months. Being grateful for what we have achieved is important in setting the stage for planning what comes next.

Your Turn to Take Action, Day 15:

Complete your review of the past twelve months. This is not the time to be humble! Be excited for your successes and honest about what needs to change in order to achieve your goals for the next twelve months.

Day 16—Creating a Yearly Plan

A great way to help you figure out your goals is to go through a visualization exercise and imagine what you have accomplished or lived through in twelve months. My suggestion would be to have someone read this to you, so that you can close your eyes and really feel and believe that it's twelve months from today. Before you begin, put yourself in a state of gratitude by reminding yourself of three things you are grateful for right at this moment. Then allow your mind to be open to creating a magical vision of what the next twelve months will bring.

Close your eyes. Imagine that it's exactly twelve months from today. You are surrounded by your family and friends. You are asked to share your biggest successes of the year, and also to share some of the greatest challenges you have overcome. First, think back on the fun times you enjoyed, the trips you took, the adventures that came your way. Did you attend a destination of your dreams? How many vacations did you take? Where did you go? Who was with you?

Next, take a look at your family. How much time did you spend with your immediate family? Not enough or more than enough? What about your extended family? Was there a family reunion? Did your family grow in size, maybe a new baby or child or even a grand-baby? What about your spiritual family? Were you involved in your church or spiritual group? Perhaps you joined a meditation circle or attended yoga classes? What did you do to tap into a higher power?

Take a look at your financial statement for the past twelve months, does it make you smile? Did you achieve your financial goals, either in your business or job? What about your net worth, did it increase? Were you promoted or did you land your dream job? If you're a business owner, did you grow your business and increase your client base? Did you win any awards or receive special recognition?

How about personal development and personal leadership? Was this a priority for you? What kinds of books did you read or audio books did you listen to? Were there any specific courses you took? What about a retreat or workshop? Did you carve out time to recharge your batteries, or simply go, go, go until you ran out of steam?

Now take a look at your body. Are you happy with what you see? Have you reached your optimal weight and health? How often did you visit the doctor's office? Or did you spend your visits with alternative practitioners such as chiropractors, massage therapists, naturopaths, osteopaths, and holistic nutritionists? What about your exercise routine? Did you have a specific weekly routine? What kinds of exercise did you enjoy? Were you entered in any kinds of competitions—maybe a 5k, 10k or a 21k half marathon? Was this the year you entered a triathlon or another type of extreme physical challenge? Did you push your physical limits to a new level or stay at the same healthy place? Maybe you overcame an injury and worked your way back to fitness. Are you proud of your health at the end of the year?

Finally, take a look at how your lifestyle changed. Did you move into the home of your dreams? Or finish the renovations on the house you already love? How about replacing a vehicle? Maybe something with more space for a larger family? Or something sporty for the empty nester? Were you able to relax at the end of each month, knowing that there would be more than enough money to cover all of the necessities? Did you give back more than the previous year? How about your time? Did you shift to part-time work or maybe even quit your job? Did you invest in yourself and your kids, financially? Were you able to open up new money channels, and allow more abundance into your life?

Now that you have lived through the next year in your mind, you are ready to write down your goals. Using the same format as the year in review, start with the areas of improvement you filled in from the last chapter, to begin formulating your goals for the next twelve months. Fill in no more than three specific goals for each section below or visit 30daysofgratitudebook.com for a downloadable PDF (there is another copy in Appendix D as well).

Category	3 Specific Goals	Month You Achieve This Goal
Business or work		
Family		
Health & Fitness		
Lifestyle		
Spirituality		
Education & Personal Growth		

The clearer you are with your goals, the more likely they are to be realized. Adding a month and a date to when you will complete your goal adds a concrete timeline as well. Here are a few examples of how to write your goals:

1. <u>I want to lose weight and get fit</u>. This is a start but it's not specific enough. Try this instead:
    I am releasing 20 lbs of weight by June, 2013 and have worked my way up to running three times a week for thirty minutes at a time.

2. <u>I make $100,000</u>. Yes, more specific, but try this:
    In the next twelve months, I create at least $100,000 of gross income in my business by increasing the level of service I am providing to my clients and focusing on working with key clients that I can serve best.

3. <u>Weekly date night with my partner</u>. How can we be more specific with this type of goal?
    Starting in January, I plan one date night a week with my partner. By Wednesday of the week prior, I will have our date night planned and confirmed for Saturday evening.

Once you have completed your goals for the next twelve months, print and post a copy of your goals in a place you can see them daily. Saving them on your computer or simply writing them in the book is not enough. Neither is hiding them in a drawer. Your goals should make you a little nervous and nudge you out of your comfort zone! Seeing them daily will help you to become more comfortable and confident that you are able to achieve them. When you cross off one of your goals, take a moment to be grateful for what you have achieved.

Your Turn to Take Action, Day 16:

Today is a great day to create your plan for the next twelve months. If you've already created a plan for this year, take time to update it. Our goals change throughout the year, so it's important to review them. Make sure you revise your list after you've achieved some of your goals and post an updated list. Also, if you're having trouble being specific with your goals, feel free to share them on our Facebook page and I'll check in regularly to offer you some feedback.

Day 17—Focus on the Next 90 Days

When you feel like you have too many things on your plate and have trouble focusing, use some of the strategies from earlier lessons in the book to get yourself back on track. This includes removing negative influences from your life, being happy in this moment, and giving thanks for the incredible people who surround you. This next chapter is about being focused for 90 days at a time.

> *If you go to work on your goals, your goals will go to work on you.*
> *If you go to work on your plan, your plan will go to work on you.*
> *Whatever good things we build end up building us.*—Jim Rohn

Now that you've created a plan for the next twelve months, I recommend you break that down into 90 day (quarterly) periods to make it easier to focus on your goals on a daily basis. It can sometimes feel overwhelming when you have a list of goals a mile long and aren't sure where to start—let alone achieve any of them!

A great way to keep your focus is to choose your **3 Most Important Goals** for the next twelve months. To paraphrase Darren Hardy, publisher of *Success Magazine*:

What would it take to have your BEST year ever? What are your **3 Most Important Goals**?

1. _____

2. _____

3. _____

Often, if we achieve our **3 Most Important Goals**, the rest of our goals will fall into place more easily. For example, if you reach your income goal, your lifestyle goals are also more likely to be achieved. And if you focus on one health goal, such as achieving your optimal weight, it will be easier to train for your first 5 k, or get in shape for an extreme race like Tough Mudder.

Now that you have your **3 Most Important Goals** for the year, what do these goals look like over the next 90 days? What daily actions are needed in order to achieve these goals?

This is called a Key Daily Behaviour (KDB): If your goal is to increase your income and you are a business owner, your KDB is to meet two new people or find at least two new clients/prospects every day.

What is my Key Daily Behaviour for each of my **3 Most Important Goals**?

1. _____
2. _____
3. _____

As you build your 90 day plan, it's important to make note of what your Key Daily Behaviours are. You can create a spreadsheet to track your KDB at the end of each day. Simply place a check in the square if you did it. At the end of each week, it's easy to see whether you are on track or not. Visit <u>30daysofgratitudebook. com</u> for a PDF tracking sheet you can download, or copy the one found in Appendix D.

The next step is to look at your **3 Most Important Goals** and determine what milestones you would have to achieve in the next 90 days in order to reach your goal. If your timeline for your goal is 90 days, it is critical to break it down into monthly and weekly milestones. This makes it so much easier to stay on track. Whether you use a paper daily planner or an electronic calendar, everything goes into **one** plan so that nothing is missed. You can create appointments or tasks that have reminder alarms. If you are using a paper planner, work backwards from your goal date and create written reminders of upcoming tasks and milestones so that they don't sneak up on you (as they tend to do).

Your Key Daily Behaviours and 90 day goals should be posted where you can see them. This will also serve as a reminder of what you've got to be doing daily. If you are an entrepreneur, it may be a challenge to remain focused on the actions that truly increase your sales and revenue. You may even sit down at your desk some days and not even know where to start—which can lead to inaction or wasted actions (such as hanging out on Facebook). Since you've got your Key Daily Behaviours posted, make sure these are cleared off your plate first thing in the morning or as quickly as possible.

Finally, another tip to stay focused is to build your weekly plan on Sunday evenings, including a to-do list for the week. Plan your week around your **3 Most Important Goals** and build your weekly to-do list from there. This is a good idea whether you are an employee, entrepreneur or business owner, parent or student. Planning your weekly success and writing it down leads to more success over time. As you use these tips and strategies, remember to be grateful for each step you take, as it is getting you closer and closer to realizing your vision.

Your Turn to Take Action, Day 17:

Here is a summary of what I do to stay focused:

- Every 90 days (quarterly) I review my yearly goals, check in on my **3 Most Important Goals** and plan for the next 90 days. I post a copy of the next 90 day plan in my office. If you work with a team, this can be done with a group.
- Sunday nights, for about thirty minutes, I take the time to plan my week. I use my white board to post my three goals for the week (smaller goals that will lead to the **3 Most Important Goals**). I also share my goals with my mentor.
- Finally, I create a to-do list to start my week and review my KDB.
- Daily, I review my list and cross things off. If something has been carried over for days or even weeks, I will put it on the top of the next list and (gulp!) do it first thing the next day.

I encourage you to use some of these actions to help you stay focused on achieving your **3 Most Important Goals** for the next twelve months.

Day 18—The Value of a Mentor

One of the things I am most grateful for are the incredible mentors in my life. A mentor can be many things: a coach, a guide, a counsellor, or a source of inspiration. Furthermore, a mentor does not have to be someone that you are in personal contact with. Most of the great mentors I have connected with have shared their knowledge through books, audio books or videos. Mentors play a key role when it comes to building our daily gratitude habits and many of the ideas shared in this book have been inspired by my own mentors.

Why would you want to have a mentor as a part of your journey? The art of mentoring can be traced back through ancient history; it can be found today in many different religious and spiritual practices, in addition to apprenticeship programs. There are many ways to define a mentor. To me, they are someone who is considered an expert in a certain area, and he or she is willing to share their knowledge freely with others. This communication of expertise can be done in various ways: in person; through books or audio books; at live seminars; or through video or teleconferencing programs. The most effective mentors are willing to give without expecting anything in return. They also lead with gratitude and love. What I have found is that most great mentors have also been mentored themselves, and by sharing their knowledge with others, they are paying it forward.

How do you go about finding a mentor? To begin, take a look at the most successful people in your chosen field. Then look for mentors in personal and spiritual development, as this is an important part of any successful journey. Additionally, many great mentors can be found in historical figures such as Abraham Lincoln, Benjamin Franklin and Andrew Carnegie. Once you've chosen a few mentors, begin by studying their published material. Jim Rohn was one of the first mentors I discovered. Rohn shares his insights to success in a simple, concrete way, and has inspired millions world-wide with his rags-to-riches story. He has also inspired many of the other mentors I have studied, including Darren Hardy, Tony Robbins and John C. Maxwell. These great mentors all understand and share the value of daily gratitude practices, as I mentioned in Day 2.

Should the opportunity arise to hear one of your mentors speak at an event, do what it takes to be there and find a way to meet them in person. I am very grateful to have spent time with Denis Waitley on many occasions, and to have built a friendship with this incredible mentor. I recently also had the chance to meet Darren Hardy at an event. I arrived early for his training session, so I could meet him in person. Hardy's father had passed away only days earlier, so we were all extremely grateful that he kept his commitment and attended the event. I learned a lot that day, not only from his presentation, but from his example of commitment.

There are other ways to connect with a mentor. Sometimes, you may have something to offer a mentor, and they will trade you their valuable time in exchange. John C. Maxwell shared a story about a member of his church who offered to do weekly errands for him, so that he would be free to spend more time working on speaking and writing. This turned into a decade-long relationship. If you're not ready to ask a celebrity or famous author for their time, start with someone in your neighborhood instead. Want to have the most successful dental practice in town? Invite a successful local dentist to lunch and ask if he or she will share some of their ideas with you. Instead of looking at them as your competition, choose to lead with gratitude; be appreciative to have such an expert in your community to learn from.

I feel very blessed to work with one of my best friends, Leanne Grechulk, in a network marketing business together. As I mentioned in the introduction, she has become one of the most influential mentors in my life, and I am very grateful to have the opportunity to learn from her successes, and also her mistakes. Paying it forward is an important part of the circle of mentorship, and I have had the honour to mentor many incredible men and women over the past seven years. This is one of the reasons that I chose network marketing as my career. I have always loved coaching and teaching others, and have found that in this career I am given the opportunity to do both on a daily basis. As Robert Kyosaki said in *The Business of The 21ˢᵗ Century*:

Network marketing tends to develop the type of leader who influences others by being a great teacher, teaching others to fulfill their life's dreams by teaching others to go for their dreams.

Throughout my life, I have been influenced by many different mentors, and have given back by taking what I have learned and mentoring others on their leadership journey. Do not to underestimate the influence of a powerful mentor on your career and your life. If you're not sure where to start, take a look at the recommended mentor list in Appendix B. These mentors have all influenced my life in a very positive way.

Your Turn to Take Action, Day 18:

Personal and spiritual mentors are an important part of your journey. Take some time to find a mentor who has similar values, and who has accomplished some (or all) of the things you aspire to achieve. Think back to your vision board, your goals and your five year vision. Who has already accomplished these things? A mentor can be a great guide and advisor, who helps you stay on track when you feel like things aren't working. By checking in with your mentor on a regular basis, you'll be able to tell whether you are keeping up with your gratitude habits. The best part about working with a mentor is that you are never alone, and you always have someone rooting for your success!

Day 19—Creating Connections

Creating connections is about building a network of people that you can rely on. It all starts by building relationships and learning to trust each other. By leading with integrity and gratitude when creating connections, you will be able build trust much more quickly. In my experience, building networks is an essential part of owning a business, and helps advance your career, regardless of your trade. We also rely on word-of-mouth referrals for virtually everything in our personal lives. This chapter focuses on becoming a better networker—a skill that is essential for you to realize your vision and live out your purpose. It is through expanding our networks and our circle of influence that we are able to achieve our goals.

Networking and creating connections is truly about giving and gratitude. Be grateful for the new people you meet, for the relationships you create, and for the referrals you receive. Having spent the last several years building a solid and extensive network, I'd like to share some of my tips on how to build relationships with integrity and trust. My first tip is to act with the intention of giving first and without any expectation of receiving anything in return. When we make the conversation about the other person, not ourselves, it becomes easier to overcome one of the biggest challenges when meeting someone new: how to start a conversation. My favorite is to ask, how may I help you? Additionally, here are more great conversation starters: What brings you here today? Why did you choose your business or line of work? What do love most about your job or business? What do you like to do for fun on the weekends? What is the biggest challenge you are facing today in your business or personal life?

Make sure you take the time to actively listen, without trying to solve their problems immediately, or formulate your own reply while they are speaking.

My next tip is to remember their name. This is a skill that can be improved if it's something you have trouble with. First, repeat their name a few times within the first few minutes of the conversation. Furthermore, you can create a mental picture of their name by asking how they spell it; then, create an accurate picture or visual association in your mind. Remembering a new friend's name shows respect and integrity, as you have made a conscious effort to remember who they are. Not to worry if you have forgotten someone's name, just ask them the next time you see them. It's better to be honest about forgetting than pretending you do know it!

After you've created a connection, then exchange information. If you carry a business or contact card, ensure your name and correct contact information are listed: first and last name, phone number, email address and website if you have one. Carry extra cards in your purse, briefcase, wallet, or diaper bag, as you never know when you will meet new people. Don't have a personal card? Carry a small notebook with you so that you can record people's information when you connect; alternatively, you can enter new contact information directly into your phone. If your phone is connected to Facebook, add them as a friend and their profile photo will help you to remember their name and face.

Whether you meet someone at a networking event, a playground or at the grocery store, it's important to be genuine in your interaction. The last thing you want is for them to feel like you are trying to sell them something or get something from them. Ask yourself this, how may I be of service to this person? When you add more value to people's lives, your perceived value also increases; therefore, more people will be attracted into your life. This is one of the reasons that network-building helps you to achieve your goals. As your network and circle of influence grows, it becomes easier for the "how" of your vision to be realized.

Another great way to grow your circle of influence is to become a master networker by introducing people to each other. To begin with, when you are at an event (networking, social gathering, children's play group) where you know several people, take the time to introduce two people whom you believe have a shared connection. For example, perhaps two people come from the same hometown, speak the same second language, have kids the same age, share a profession or are in complimentary professions (such as a real estate agent and a mortgage broker), or attended the same college or university. This shows people that you've been listening to them, and also shows your ability to create connections.

Similarly, when you meet accountants, real estate brokers, mortgage brokers and social media/web experts—find out what sets them apart from the crowd, as chances are you already know half a dozen people with the same profession. Be genuinely interested in learning about them and their strengths. And finally, follow up within 48 hours. The fortune is in the follow up! After exchanging cards, write a quick note on the back as a reminder of who they are and why you wanted to reconnect with them; this could include giving a referral or offering to help. You can do the same thing by adding a note on your phone or in your notebook. If you've promised them some information or have a referral to give them, respond within 48-72 hours. Wait any longer and the relationship may be more difficult to cultivate, since you may have already broken their trust. Equally important, when someone contacts you after you've met them, take the time to return their call or respond to their email. It's hard to expect others to respond to you, if you don't do the same for others.

If you're looking for a short cut to realizing your vision, creating solid connections and adding value to other people's lives will most definitely help. Expressing gratitude for your new connections and being grateful for referrals you receive will pave the way to success.

Your Turn to Take Action, Day 19:

Challenge yourself to meet two new people this week and to create a connection. It can be anywhere in your life. Reach out and start a conversation with a stranger. If you're a business owner, visit a networking group or event. A great place to meet new people is via Meetup.com where you can connect with like-minded people. Whether it be for a hobby, sports, your kids, business networking, games, learning new languages—there are endless opportunities to create connections.

Day 20—Building Teams

You are the average of the five people you spend the most time with.
—Jim Rohn

Now that you've learned the value of creating connections to help achieve your goals, the next step is to build teams. A team can also be a network, a support group and even your family. These are the people that will help you to grow and blossom in life. They are also the ones who will put you back on track when you've lost your way. Your team can be filled with mentors, friends and coaches, who hold you accountable to being the best person you can be. Gratitude and daily gratitude practices are what allow you to build teams of incredible people in your life. As explained in the previous chapter, the more attractive you become to the world (I'm not talking about plastic surgery here!), the more people will be attracted to you. A solid foundation based on gratitude, faith, and integrity allows more and more people to find their way into your life. My early experience in building friendships and teams was not easy, but I am now surrounded by incredible people daily. So don't worry if you're feeling alone right now, that can change!

Growing up, I never seemed to fit in. Back in grade school, there were only a few girls in my class and I didn't get along with them, so I was left out. I lost my temper on many occasions and fought with many people at school. Like many kids, I was teased and bullied throughout the years. I tried so hard to fit in by doing what I thought would please other people. This meant participating in everything possible, such as school sports teams, band, choir, the school musical, science fair, and public speaking; you name it, I was in it! Yet, none of these things really mattered to anyone else. In the end, I still never really fit in and lived most of my life without having a team or support network. What I have found now, is that leading with anger only leads to more of the same. If I had learned to lead with love and gratitude first, some of the outcomes may have been different. As a child, it can be difficult to understand this, and I have devoted a further chapter on the importance of teaching our children gratitude habits.

As I moved on to high school, I thought (as most kids do) that this would be a great opportunity to start over and make new friends. Again, I wanted to fit in so badly, and I tried so hard to be a part of the *team*. For me, that was the music crowd. Once again, I joined everything: choir, band, the school musical, and cabaret nights. I even participated in musical theatre outside of school. This is where I met my only true friend from my high school years, my best friend Lee-Anne. She was able to see beyond my faults, as I lead with my ego and placed myself and my goals before others. Looking back now, I can see that I believed if I was really good at something, people would like me. I realize now that building relationships doesn't have much to do with me, it's about getting to know the other person, their likes and dislikes, and caring about who they are. It's learning to give from a place other than the ego.

After high school I started university, where I eventually ended up studying Kinesiology. It seemed like once again, I would have trouble fitting in. One of the biggest challenges for me was that I was unable to run or do many sports because of knee injuries (from a childhood career as a competitive gymnast); this was difficult to overcome in such a sport focused degree. Despite this, I spent a few summers working at the sports camp for children. This was the place where I felt the most ostracized, as I could not run and there were many running activities in which I was not able to participate. I was teased and ridiculed, which was very difficult for me. Once again, I found myself trying too hard to fit in, and if I had just been myself, I probably would have fared much better. I was already starting to learn about gratitude though. One of the things I did to try to overcome not fitting in, was posting a Thought of the Day on the bulletin board (anonymously). This was how I gave back, by sharing something positive, even though I found things to be difficult on the outside. I was slowly learning to lead with my heart, rather than my ego.

As I left school and moved into the workforce, I began to build better relationships with people, and my circle of friends started to grow. The biggest turning point for me was when I started my business seven years ago. I finally began connecting with people as my authentic self. For me, finding a group of like-minded people with similar goals and dreams made it easier to be myself and allowed me to create true friendships. Coincidentally, as I started to build these new relationships, I also started my first gratitude journal. I've come to realize that my own daily gratitude processes helped me to attract more wonderful people into my life.

Since that time, I have been building different teams into the many parts of my life. I finally feel like I fit in, and I really enjoy being surrounded by so many great people. Here are just a few examples of the types of teams who surround me:

- Business building team—the people I coach and mentor, as well as my own mentors and other business partners.

- Services team—the people I turn to when I personally need a specific product or service; I would also refer these services people to someone else if they asked for guidance.

- Mommy team—the moms I have met through my daughter. We meet for programs and play dates, and we share our **real** mommy stories together.

- Networking team—A team of business people I meet with regularly in a networking meeting. We take the time to get to know each other's business, product or service, and refer business to each other whenever possible. We also mastermind and work on creating solutions to different business challenges we are facing.

- Spiritual team—Personally, this is found at my church. I feel amazing when I come home after teaching Sunday school and listening to the service.

- My friends and family team—This is the foundation for my support network. I have a very close knit family and they are the number one priority for me. And I value friendships with family and friends very highly. I would not have been able to finish this book without their support, most of all, my sister Sophie.

The best advice I can give is to surround yourself with the best people you know. People you cannot wait to see and make you smile when you see them, and people who have your best interest at heart. And perhaps most importantly, people who are honest and direct with you when you need it most. Out of all of these different teams in your life, who are the five people you spend the most time with? Are they supportive on your journey to live an extraordinary life? Do they support your gratitude practices or make fun of them? Do they rally around you when you've had a success or let it go by without taking note? This core team of five is the most important of all. Take a look around you—are you grateful for those who are standing closest to you right now?

Your Turn to Take Action, Day 20:

Take a look at the different teams in your life. Are they supporting you? How do you feel after you've spent time with them, better or worse? Start off by being grateful for all of the wonderful people in your life, whether it's only one person or a hundred. If most of the people you are spending time with don't make you feel very good, it's time to start building new and more supportive teams. Use the strategies in the previous chapter to help you meet new people. This is not something that will happen overnight, but I encourage you to shift your time spent with negative people, and focus on finding more positive and encouraging people to spend time with. As you build more teams with like-minded people, you will find that living from a place of gratitude has become second nature and that it's easy to lead with love every single day.

As we wrap up the second section, I hope you've begun creating a plan to live your vision. It takes time to get through many of the tasks and planning exercises in this section, so it's okay if it takes longer than ten days. Revisit this section on a yearly basis, as you prepare your plan for the following year.

The next section is about even more amazing ways that gratitude can change your life. I will be talking about creating an abundance mentality throughout this section, as I've discovered that gratitude and abundance go hand-in-hand. Being grateful for what you already have is the foundation, and allowing more abundance into your life is the next step. I will also share fun ways to be grateful for your own success, and how to be grateful for other people's successes. Finally, through more personal stories you'll learn about using the law of attraction to attract your perfect partner, and the role that faith plays alongside gratitude.

Section 3

More Amazing Ways Gratitude Can Change Your Life

Happiness cannot be traveled to, owned, earned,
worn or consumed. Happiness is the spiritual experience of living
every minute with love, grace, and gratitude.

Denis Waitley

Day 21—Two Very Important Lists

This is such a fun exercise to do! I did this several years ago with my family; we all completed our lists and sat down together to share them. This is also a wonderful way to get to know people.

The first list is the <u>Personal Success List,</u> which works best when written, so grab a new notebook and start writing out your successes in life. Go all the way back to learning how to walk, to ride a bike, to swim; include things like graduating from high school—every little success you can remember. You goal is to reach **100 items** on your list. Continue working on the list until you've reached one hundred. This activity is a great way to look back and be grateful for where you've been, and what you've accomplished.

The second part of this exercise is the <u>Lifetime of Gratitude</u> list: being grateful for ten things in each decade of your life. If you're in your 50s, it would look like this:

- 0-10 years old: 10 things I am most grateful for.
- 11-20 years old: 10 things I am most grateful for.
- 21-30 years old: 10 things I am most grateful for.
- 31-40 years old: 10 things I am most grateful for.
- 40-now: 10 things I am most grateful for.

To make this even more fun, get together with your family, your team or your friends, and have everyone complete these exercises beforehand. Take turns sharing from both of your lists. Turn this into a game by choosing a few things from each decade or from your success list, and writing them on a slip of paper that goes into a central bowl. Take turns pulling slips of paper from the bowl and guessing who wrote them.

> *Your Turn to Take Action, Day 21:*
>
> Find a new notebook and start your list! Aim to reach one hundred successes as quickly as possible, while you have the momentum. Once you've reached at least a hundred (you are welcome to go beyond!) use that list to create your <u>Lifetime of Gratitude</u> list. Want to share the love? Invite four to five people to complete these same exercises and get together to share, using one of the activities outlined above.

Day 22—Create a Dream Book

Creating a dream book goes beyond the vision board, because you can include more pictures, ideas and experiences. A dream book is typically more detailed than a vision board and also starts from a place of gratitude. There are several ways this can be done; here are some options:

- Journal
- Spiral notebook
- Photo album
- Scrapbook
- Power Point presentation, using slides as your pages

Much like a vision board, you collect images of the items you desire, the places you would like to live, where you'd like to travel, cars you'd like to drive, etc. You have a lot more freedom and space with a dream book, so collect as many as you like. You'll be creating a visual story, with a few words, that describes your ideal life. The goal is that when you share your dream book with someone else, they may actually believe you've been there and done that!

On the first page, start with gratitude:

I am so happy and grateful now that I have ….

Include a photo of yourself, smiling and happy, and decorate it with things that represent gratitude and self-love. On the next page, include one photo or image and write what you have accomplished in the present tense. For example, if your goal is to hike to Mount Everest Base Camp, paste an image of this in your book. Underneath the image write: *I am enjoying the view from the Base Camp of Mount Everest.* Add a picture of yourself to the image using Photoshop, or simply cut and paste your photo to the image of Mount Everest Base Camp.

What is your dream car? Head down to the car dealership, and take the car for a test drive. Rather than taking a brochure, take a picture of yourself sitting in the car. Place it in your dream book and underneath it write: *I love driving my new Porsche 911* (or whatever happens to be your dream car).

Once you've finished your dream book, leave it out on the coffee table or bedside table so that you look at it daily. The more often you see yourself living out your dreams, the more likely they are to appear in reality. And the best part is they usually appear in ways you least expected, so let go of any pre-conceived notions about how you'll achieve them.

What does a thought look like? Just look around you, right now... to see yours.—Mike Dooley

---

Your Turn to Take Action, Day 22:

Another way to show immediate gratitude for the life you are creating is to make a dream book. This is something you can start today and continue to add to as your dreams and goals change or are realized. Don't have enough to fill a book? Start anyhow. Create the photo album of your life as you see it in your mind and it will come to life in our physical word.

Day 23—How to be Happy for Others' Successes

I have an abundance mentality: When people are genuinely happy at the successes of others, the pie gets larger.—Stephen Covey

As I shared in the introduction, jealousy has been a big part of my struggle towards leading a life of gratitude. Jealousy is defined as: resentment against a rival, a person enjoying success or advantage, etc., or against another's success or advantage itself[1]. This emotion can be very toxic and debilitating for many people, and I have experienced this personally. Being jealous does not allow you to be truly happy for other people's successes, and it may also lead to sabotaging your own success.

How do you feel when someone at work is promoted before you? Or when an award you desired went to a friend or colleague? What if someone was recognized for something you had also accomplished, but you failed to be acknowledged? How would you feel about friends who bought their first home when you're still living in an apartment? On the outside, most people would be happy for others and congratulate them. The difficulty is dealing with the emotions on the inside—not necessarily the surface emotions, but how you really feel about it. Have you ever had any these thoughts?

> *I should have been promoted first, I work so hard and I've been here longer.*
> *I deserve the award. I should have been chosen. Let me talk to the judges and we'll fix this.*

---

[1] http://dictionary.reference.com/

> *I did the same thing last month! How come I wasn't recognized?*
> *Why wasn't my name included?*
> *I make just as much money as they do, how can they afford a*
> *house?*

This type of thinking can become toxic to both your mind and body over time, particularly if you do not have a healthy way of releasing your frustrations. As I explained in the introduction, I personally experienced this in my business several years ago. Truth be told, jealousy is one of the emotions I have struggled with the most. Since I thrive on being recognized for my accomplishments, for a long time I wasn't able to be truly happy for other people's successes. I always felt like it took something away from me if someone else was recognized instead of me. Being an honour roll student all the way through primary and secondary school was when this first started—it became crucial for me to see my name printed on the honour roll list. When I didn't make the honour roll in my first year of university, I was devastated. I made sure I was on that list for the next three years, no matter what it took, and many of my relationships with my peers were strained because of my need to always be at the top. I also loved the feeling of winning awards and being recognized for different accomplishments.

In my last year of elementary school, there was an award given out at the end of the year for best all-around athlete. I knew that part of the criteria was to be on as many school teams as possible. That year I was on eight different teams. I knew the competition was close with a friend of mine. In the end, we were both given the award. On the outside I was happy for her, but on the inside, I believed I alone deserved all of the recognition. And my friend didn't care either way, she was happy with or without the recognition.

If you have ever struggled with jealousy, you can relate to these stories. Recently, I have discovered a few strategies to help avoid jealousy, or how to deal with it and move on when it occurs. First, when it comes to recognition, I realize now that there is no limited amount of recognition. There is enough to go around for everyone, not just me! Furthermore, I learned that it feels fantastic to give others recognition—sometimes even more than receiving it. Learning to be more humble is also helpful to avoid feeling jealous. My mentor, Leanne Grechulk, is one of the most humble people I know. She is recognized often and in so many ways, but it's almost as if she doesn't notice. What she does very well is give recognition to others. She is one of the most generous and grateful people I know, and she has taught me a lot about showing gratitude when others are recognized.

You see, in the final analysis, it is between you and God, it was never between you and them anyways.—Mother Theresa

That's the truth. Jealousy is an emotion that is about me versus you. Take out the competition with someone else, and you've taken out jealousy. If you are able to focus on your own personal journey and not worry about others, jealousy will no longer be an issue. I find that this is the best way to let go of this emotion. Your success takes absolutely nothing away from mine. We live in a world of abundance, and in the next chapter I will talk about how to see that abundance every day. There is more than enough success for everyone! Remind yourself of that next time someone is promoted, wins an award, or publishes a book before you. Your successes will also be celebrated when the time comes, so why not join the celebration for someone else? Take a moment to be grateful that they have shown you the way. Chances are you'll learn something from their successes and failures.

Your Turn to Take Action, Day 23:

What does being humble mean to you? Take a moment to figure out if there are places in your life where you could be more humble. Who can you celebrate today? If you have employees or a team, take a few minutes to personally recognize their work or a recent accomplishment. Make it specific to them and keep it positive. You'll be surprised at how far a little recognition can go. And next time you're the runner-up, take a deep breath, smile and make sure you're the first in line to congratulate the winner.

Day 24—Seeing Abundance Everywhere

Learning to see abundance everywhere is a skill that helps you to be grateful throughout your day. First, let me ask you this: When you see a penny or coin on the ground, do you pick it up? Or would you only stoop down for a larger sum of money, such as a bill or larger denomination coin? Something I learned from T. Harv Eker's *Millionaire Mind Intensive Program* is to pick up ALL of the money you see laying on the ground! This is the Universe telling you that there is money everywhere—it is a sign that you are attracting more money. And if you don't pick it up, you're basically telling the Universe that you don't want to attract more money! Then when you do pick it up: give it a kiss and out loud, say *Thank you, Thank you, Thank you*!! I love doing this. It's a simple way to attract more money into your life and to show gratitude for FREE money! I will pick up the dirtiest pennies and kiss them too. Why not? Do the same if you find surprise pocket money—you know when you put on your spring coat for the first time and you find $5 in the pocket—yes that's surprise pocket money. *Thank you, Thank you and Thank you!*

According to Jim Rohn:

> "...*fruitfulness and abundance mean—to go to work on producing more than you need for yourself so you can begin blessing others, blessing your nation and blessing your enterprise. Once abundance starts to come, once someone becomes incredibly productive, it's amazing what the numbers turn out to be. But to begin this incredible process of blessing, it often starts with the act of thanksgiving and gratitude, being thankful for what you*

already have and for what you've already done. Begin the act of thanksgiving today and watch the miracles flow your way."

There are so many ways that nature shows us abundance. Does grass struggle to grow? In many climates, it grows so quickly that people have to mow their lawns weekly. How about the leaves on the trees, do they not seem uncountable? A field of wildflowers has no end. Plant one tomato seed and you'll get a whole plant with many, many tomatoes. Nature is abundant and has no difficulty multiplying; in fact, it is always fighting for life and looking to expand wherever it can. Ever had ivy growing on the side of your house? It's nearly impossible to stop! As you go through your day, take a look around outside. Take a moment to be grateful for the abundance of nature and all of nature's creatures. Humans also have unlimited capacities for growth and abundance. We are an inseparable part of nature and there are no limits to what we can achieve.

I love walking outside. It is my exercise of choice these days. I used to be a runner and a tri-athlete, but have taken time off the intensive training I once did for Ironman triathlons. In my days of training for triathlons, I had many opportunities to train outside and I often found money! It also gave me an opportunity to appreciate nature. Rather than listening to music while running, I liked to listen to the sounds around me and observe my surroundings. If you are a runner or a walker, go outside next time without your iPod and enjoy the abundance of nature. Be grateful that you can run or walk outside. Be grateful for your healthy body that allows you to do this. Be grateful for the sun, the rain, the snow, the wind, or whatever conditions you experience. Take this one workout to reconnect with your body and with nature.

Your Turn to Take Action, Day 24:

Get outside! No matter what time of year it is, take ten minutes today to just be outside. Connect with nature. Observe abundance. Smile at the thought of how limitless we all are. And next time you see a penny, pick it up, kiss it and yell THANK YOU, THANK YOU, THANK YOU!!! People may give you strange looks, but the Universe is listening.

Day 25—Gratitude and the Law of Attraction

Living in gratitude daily is part of what helps the law of attraction bring all that you desire into your life. I first learned about the law of attraction from the movie *The Secret*. Basically, the law of attraction states that you attract into your life what you are thinking about most. Find yourself thinking about getting out of debt and you'll attract more debt into your life. Thinking about moving into a new home? The more specific you are about the image of your home in your mind, the more rapidly it will appear in your life. However, the law of attraction does not work all on its own; being in a state of gratitude and having positive emotions is essential for attracting what you desire. All of the lessons shared so far in this book will help you to use the law of attraction to create the life you desire. One of the lessons I learned from *The Secret* was being specific about what you want, just like picking from a catalogue. The best way to show you this is to share the story of how I attracted my husband and perfect partner into my life, using the law of attraction, daily gratitude and faith.

In March 2007, I was dealing with some personal challenges and needed to spend some time away in order to find some clarity and direction. I packed up my car and set out for a six hour drive into the mountains of the Poconos. I brought along nine self-development books and my journal. No laptop, cell phone, TV or movies. I spent five days walking in nature, building fires, meeting strangers, reading and writing in my journal. I took notes on the books I read and I made long lists of all of the things I wanted in my life. Part of that list included what I was looking for in a partner. I took all of the things that had not worked in my previous relationships, and asked for the opposite. I was fairly specific, right down to *"I want a partner who is between 5'10" and 6'2" tall, with dark hair and blue eyes"*. I filled five pages of my journal with my "order".

When I came home from the trip, refreshed and renewed, I put the journal aside and rarely looked at it. But I often imagined my dream house with my partner and our kids. I could never really see his face clearly, but he was tall, with dark hair and for some reason, always wearing a white shirt. I had read somewhere that time doesn't really exist and that everything in our lives happens at the same time, just on alternate planes. So I used to imagine our life together, happening right now, on a different plane. I had fun with it, and I didn't really worry about it. And I continued to write in my journal often—being grateful for my successes each day, and also tackling different challenges that came across my path.

In November 2007, I was introduced to a book called *The Law of Attraction*, by Michael Losier. I had read dozens of books on personal development that year, but this one was unique in that it was a workbook. There are some very specific exercises you can do in the book, in order to send the most accurate message out into the Universe. On November 25th, I wrote my Desire Statement to attract my ideal partner, and came up with a one page summary of what I was looking for. For example, he had to live within a one hour drive, be fluently bilingual in French & English, be open to a relationship (I wasn't interested in dating), and be affectionate and loving. The following week, I was out running with a friend and mentioned that I was going to spend New Year's Eve with my boyfriend. Keep in mind that I wasn't even dating anyone at this time!

In the meantime, the stars were lining up for my husband as well. Not long before we met, he had been living about thirty minutes away from me, but had been commuting to a job several hours in the other direction. There was no way for us to meet! Fortunately, he was laid off from his job and ended up getting a new job five minutes from where I lived. Of course that didn't mean we would meet.

So how did we finally connect? A good friend whom I worked with in University found me on Facebook in September 2007. It turned out she worked just down the street from where I lived, so we met for lunch. We discussed several things, including business; one thing lead to another, and we ended up working together. This was an interesting turn of events, as I wasn't in the habit of bringing up business over lunch with people I hadn't seen in a while, I preferred to re-connect and build a relationship first. But in this case, it worked out, and because of our business alliance, I would often drop by her office at lunch time.

On December 7th, less than a month after writing my desire statement, I popped by this friend's office to lend her a copy of *The Secret* DVD. That was the day that she introduced my husband and I. I noticed right away that he was cute and tall, but we barely exchanged more than a few sentences. She connected us on Facebook, and I immediately noticed that he had been to French school and that he was bilingual. I was already excited!

Our first date was lunch at Paradiso Restaurant, a local favorite. We sat in a booth, and it was instant electricity for both of us. Needless to say, it was a great first date. On our next date, we had pretty much decided that we were going to be together—so

I thought it might be interesting to see how he stacked up to my Desire Statement:

- My ideal relationship is with a man who is looking for a committed relationship and lives within an hour drive.
- My ideal partner is only six years older or younger than I am.
- He is fluent in French and English.
- He is passionate, living his life with passion and purpose; he is working towards financial freedom.
- He enjoys being physically active.
- He can dream big and has many exciting goals for his and our lives, and he inspires me every day.

That is a summary of what was written on that Desire Statement. I didn't know all of these things about him within the first few days, but it became evident within a few months how much he fit exactly what I had been searching for. When I wrote those words down, I knew that I would meet the one who fit my desires. I never doubted it and had faith that he would come into my life. And having a strong faith is essential to help you attract what you want in your life. I'll share more about the importance having faith in the next chapter.

We are truly blessed to have a wonderful relationship. We can spend days together and still be very happy. This is the relationship I have always dreamed of—I chose not to make compromises on what I truly desired and I got it. We are open with each other, there are no secrets between us, and we support each other unconditionally. We were married on July 12, 2009, at Paradiso Restaurant, the same place as our first date. Today we live in our first dream home, with our beautiful daughter; and as a family, we express our gratitude daily for our incredible lives.

There were several key tools that I used in order to allow the law of attraction to bring me what I truly desired in my heart:

- I took the time and space to be clear about what I wanted.
- I let go and let the Universe figure out how he was going to come into my life.
- I had faith that I knew what I wanted and that I wasn't going to settle for anything else.
- I continued to be grateful for what I did have in my life at that time, even though I was going through personal challenges.

You can use these same tools to attract what it is you truly desire in your life. Whether it be your perfect partner, your dream job, your ideal business partners or your dream home, anything is possible!

Your Turn to Take Action, Day 25:

Be crystal clear on what you are looking to attract in your life. All of the skills that you have learned throughout this book will help you to stay positive and use gratitude in your daily life. If you are specifically looking to attract something or someone into your life, write out in detail (in the present tense) what it is you are looking for. Be very specific. Then let go and let God, which means that you let go of any attachments to the results or worrying about how it will happen. It will.

Day 26—The Power of Faith

It's Sunday afternoon and I've just come home from church. Two years ago, I never believed I would go to church every Sunday. Of course, I had a hard time truly believing in many things. This chapter is about the importance of faith, however you choose to find it, and why it's one of the foundations for daily gratitude and intentions.

Faith had always been somewhat of a mystery to me. Although I was baptised as a Roman-Catholic, our family did not attend church. We were the Christmas-Easter people; you know, the ones who show up on Christmas Eve and Easter Sunday? That was all I really knew about church. And I found that I had a hard time even saying the word God, let alone believing there was such a being. As I started my journey with gratitude, I became aware that in order to believe that my visions, dreams and desires would be realized on this earth, I would need to have faith in a higher power. All of the spiritual teachings I had read spoke about God or the Universe or a higher power. At that time, I felt comfortable believing in the Universe. I would let go of what I had asked for, and allow the Universe to figure out the rest. And I did have faith that it worked. After all, the Universe had allowed everything to align, albeit in unexpected ways, in order for my husband and I to meet.

Faith is the soil for planting the seeds of gratitude and abundance. If you have a strong, unwavering faith, then the soil is fertile, and your seeds of gratitude and abundance will flourish. But if your faith is not as deep or as strong, then the soil lacks nutrients and the seeds will not reach their full potential.

> *We are unlimited beings. We have no ceiling. The capabilities and the talents and the gifts and **the power that is within every single individual** that is on this planet, is unlimited*—Michael Beckwith

This quote by Rev. Michael Beckwith refers to "the power that is within every single individual". I believe he is referring to the fact that we all have God-like power within us, and having faith is what allows us to express it in unlimited ways. Dr. Wayne Dyer speaks about this in both his movie *The Shift* and the book *Wishes Fulfilled*. To paraphrase his example, when you take a whole apple pie and cut out a slice, is the slice still apple pie? Of course it is! So, if we were all created from one being, a higher power, God, The Universe, wouldn't we still hold a part of that power within each one of us? The answer is yes. And that is why faith is the foundation for all that we do.

My own faith was tested during the two years when I left my business, as explained in the introduction. I found myself going through difficult times and not knowing what to count on, or where to place my faith. It seemed that for me, having faith in the Universe was simply not enough. When my daughter was born, I had a desire to have her baptised. I called the small French Catholic church nearby to ask about her baptism. They told me I had to attend twice before they would do it. Twice seemed a bit like a cop out to me, so I started attending weekly. And I enjoyed it! The singing, the prayer, and the structure of the service all really appealed to me; I also appreciated it being French. I started to become more and more curious about the scripture we were learning about each week, as I often did not understand the passages. About ten months later, they were looking for teachers for Sunday school. I offered to help out, as I had been a French teacher and private tutor for years, with the caveat that I had not studied the Bible at all. At first, I taught once a month and another parishioner taught the rest of the time. I learned quite a bit from him as he was very knowledgeable about the Bible and the Church.

Two months later, I wrote out my goals for the year and included teaching Sunday school twice a month and studying at least one passage from the Bible each week. A few weeks later, the man I had been working with passed away quite suddenly from a heart attack. I was very upset by this loss. God, in His wisdom, had given me the opportunity to fulfill my goals as a result of this tragedy. I stepped up to the primary role at Sunday school and began teaching weekly. To prepare for the lessons, I had to learn and understand the reading beforehand. One year later, my faith is very strong and most certainly unshakable. I love going to church and teaching. It is one of the highlights of my week. I have built relationships with the students and also have found a community in my church. This is what I needed to do in order to solidify my own faith.

For you, this may not be the case. Organized religion is not for everyone, and I do not advocate this as a solution for all. Faith is such a personal thing, and whatever source you draw from for your faith is perfect. Having faith is what is most important. No matter what, the stronger your foundation is, the more solid your vision becomes.

Your Turn to Take Action, Day 26:

Where do find your faith? When a tragedy occurs, or you have failed at one of your goals, or a recession hits and your business suffers, where do you turn to? With a strong faith, you'll be able to turn inside and find unlimited power within you, which allows you to go through a difficult time and find a beautiful lesson on the other side. Are you curious about going to church? There are so many different options today; visit a few different services and find one that fits for you. And if not, that's okay. Step outside your door, the church of the Universe is always open for everyone!

Day 27—Gratitude and Kindness

How do you find time in your day to be kind to others? Do you take the time to be grateful for the people who cross your path throughout the day? Sometimes in our hectic lives we forgot to slow down and thank the people whom we interact with throughout the day. Even more alarming is that sometimes we forgot to be kind and pay gratitude to our families. Why not be the one that spreads light and kindness wherever you go? Be the one who brightens a room when you enter. Take the time to be present throughout the day so that you can give your full attention to every human being who you interact with.

How can this be done? A few simple ideas would be to start by thanking your family for the little things, for example:

- Thanking your spouse for doing chores around the house, even if you had to nag him or her to do it. And if you get into the habit of showing gratitude for the chores they do, soon enough there will be no nagging needed!
- Thanking your children for cleaning up after themselves. Sometimes we ask our children to clean-up, but forget to thank them afterwards for doing it. With small children especially, they want to know that you noticed their hard work.

It's important to be kind to the people we love. Telling them we love them, giving them hugs and smiling when we look at them. These are all ways to be kind for free! This also works well with strangers. Think about all of the people you interact with in one day: the barista at the coffee shop, the gas station attendant, the parking lot attendant, the receptionist or secretary who greets you when you walk in the office, your team, the person who serves or delivers your lunch, the mail carrier, any of the retail shop employees you may visit, the grocery store clerk, the sushi chef, the greeters, the cashiers, your teachers or children's teachers. What if you made an effort to simply smile at each one of them and say thank you? This sounds incredibly simple but we so often forget! Your smile could change someone's mood and bring joy to their day. As for hugging, I heard that you need at least twelve hugs per day for growth. Why not? Whenever possible, hug someone! I am a hugger by nature and I find myself hugging even my new networking partners within a few hours of meeting them. Sound a bit forward? Perhaps—but I always ask first and never get refused.

Beyond smiling and saying thank you, random acts of kindness are always a wonderful gift—not only to the person receiving them, but for the person who is giving them. Challenge yourself to perform three to five random acts of kindness in the next week. Here are a few suggestions to get you started:

- Pay for the person behind you in a drive-thru when getting coffee in the morning.
- Put money in an expired parking meter.
- Send flowers to a nursing home and request that they be given to someone who has no visitors.
- Donate anonymously to charity.
- Send gift certificates for Chapters or Barnes and Nobel to three networking partners, without including your card or a return address.

- Donate used books to the library.
- At the grocery store, let someone go ahead of you in line

For more inspiring ideas, take a look at the Random Acts of Kindness Foundation® online: http://www.randomactsofkindness.org/.

Being kind to others, without recognition, allows you to learn be more humble. This skill is important to have as we learn to be happy for other's successes as discussed in Day 23. What I've noticed is that the more we give without expecting anything in return, the more we increase the feelings of abundance in our lives—there is so much we can give for free and we'll never run out!

Lastly, in our world of social media, and the instant ability to share all of the details of our lives with our friends and colleagues, I feel that it's important to apply these same principles to the virtual world as well. When posting a status or a photo on Facebook or Twitter, ask yourself a few questions before hitting send:

- Is this a positive or negative message?
- Would I let my children read this message?
- How would my grandmother react?
- Could someone's feelings be hurt?
- Does this give me an uncomfortable feeling in the pit of my stomach?

As I talked about in Day 3, our words can be very powerful. Today we may feel as though we can use social media to air our dirty laundry without consequence, but the reality is that what we say and write always has an effect. It's up to you whether you add love and gratitude to the world or spread negativity.

Your Turn to Take Action, Day 27:

For the next week, make an effort to smile at everyone who crosses your path during the day—especially your family. Remember to thank them for the little things, so they know that you have noticed their efforts. Make a commitment to practice three to five random acts of kindness this week. Involve your partner and your kids; teach them about what it means to give without any recognition or acknowledgement, so that they can learn how wonderful it feels to give from the heart. Pay close attention to what you are posting on social media; be aware of the power of your words. Finally, hug everyone possible!

Day 28—Clearing Space

It's essential to clear space if you want to allow more abundance into all areas of your life. Once you have created daily gratitude habits, more and more abundance will flow into your life. If there is no space to allow it to enter, it will simply go elsewhere. Let's take a look at how you can make space.

Whether you live in an apartment, townhouse, detached home or trailer, de-cluttering is a necessity. Ever noticed that as we move into a larger home we always seem to find a way to fill *all* of the space? There is a global movement to simplify and reduce the amount of 'stuff' we have, and to keep only what we need. In my own life, I have been through this experience a few times. When I backpacked around Europe the first time, all I carried was a 55L backpack and a small day pack. A few years later, when I travelled and lived overseas for several years, I moved every few months, so I had to be able to carry everything I owned.

Even though I live in a house now, I still have the same mentality. I regularly clean out our closets and dressers, getting rid of stuff that hasn't been worn in more than one season. If two summers go by and you haven't worn it, time to get rid of it! One suggestion, if you keep 'fat' clothes in your closet, you're basically telling the Universe that you're planning to gain weight again. Love your body, love your weight and let go of the clothing that no longer fits you! Same goes for your skinny jeans from ten years ago. It's ok to pass them on to someone else who will look and feel amazing in them.

I love being able to give away clothing and other household items that we are no longer using. I feel grateful that these items served us at one time, and am glad that they are going to a new home where someone else will appreciate them. There are many charities and organizations that will pick up used clothing and other household goods right at your front door. If your closet doors aren't closing and your drawers are overflowing, it's time to let go of some things. If all of your space is filled with 'stuff' how will more abundance find its way in?

The last point I want to make regarding your home is about the front entrance. This relates to the feng shui concept of allowing energy to enter your home and flow freely. First, make sure the outside is kept clean and bright, and that your house numbers are easy to see. Second, when you enter your home, your hallway or landing should be open and bright, again to invite the energy into your home. Third, keep your entrance clear of shoes, coats and other items such as keys, mail and school bags, as this makes it easier to for people to enter and exit the home. There are many more great tips in *10 Minute Feng Shui* by Skye Alexander.

Another place to keep clean is your vehicle. This is especially important if you're looking to attract a new vehicle into your life. If you keep your vehicle clean inside and out, do the scheduled maintenance and are grateful every time you drive, your new vehicle will arrive more quickly. Think about it, if you're planning to trade your vehicle for a new one, shouldn't it be in top shape? Also, if your trunk is always full, think about the message being sent out to the Universe—no room for anything new or wonderful in here, we're already full!

Finally, how about clearing electronic space? Is your inbox always overflowing? Do you jump every time your phone dings with a new Facebook or Twitter notification? How many electronic newsletters or daily deals are you subscribed to? Clearing space in your inbox is much like clearing space in your home. You are allowing space for more positive and pleasant messages into your life by making space. Get in the habit of deleting messages after you've read them, or filing them in email folders if you wish to view them later. Also, it's nice to open your email inbox and have less than ten new messages. When I turn on my phone in the morning, I have fewer than five new messages, and one is always from Shift Happens! Daily Inspiration from Robert Holden (author of *Shift Happens!*). I read it, absorb it and immediately delete it. It's a great way to start my day.

Most of people are subscribed to anywhere from 10–100 different email newsletters and updates from various companies, real estate agents, stores, airlines—the list is endless. Here are a few suggestions on how to make it stop:

- First, take notice when you enter your email address for *anything* online. Chances are there is a box or two that is <u>automatically</u> checked off and that adds you to their email list. For example, when adding an online electronic retailer account, there were two boxes that I had to <u>uncheck</u> so that I wouldn't be added to their promos and flyers.
- Next, keep all newsletters, promos, and flyers that arrive in your inbox. Before deleting them, find the unsubscribe link and take ten seconds to unsubscribe. Likely there are only two or three that you really need to receive at all. Things that I remain subscribed to? Newsletters from Darren Hardy, Jim Rohn and Denis Waitley, Daily

Inspiration from Robert Holden, the Low GI Newsletter and Dr. Libby Weaver.

- Daily emails are the worst—especially things like WagJag or Groupon—ask yourself if you need those extra steak knives or the deal on the yoga classes. If you have time to shop online, just go directly to the sites and shop. Alternatively, follow them on their Facebook pages.

I posted a blog about how to unsubscribe from Facebook notifications, including images and detailed instructions. You can find it here: http://julieboyer.com/trouble-with-facebook-notifications/.

Your Turn to Take Action, Day 28:

To clear space in your home, start with one room at a time. Separate items into three piles: keep, donate, or toss. The goal is to have larger donate or toss piles! Connect with a local charity to arrange pick-up. Most communities also have a large household item pick-up day, so consult your community website for those dates and plan your clean-up ahead of time. For your car, empty your trunk and take your car to the auto spa. Prices range from $20-$120, depending on the amount of detailing. Lastly, start clearing out your inbox today. Archive everything that is already in there and start fresh (by archiving you don't lose anything, the messages can still be found via the search feature). When you receive a newsletter, immediately unsubscribe. If you do take the time to read it, file it or trash it after you've read it.

Day 29—Children and Gratitude

One of the greatest gifts we can teach our children is how to be grateful every day. As a parent, it can sometimes be challenging to be grateful for our children when they misbehave, push our limits, disobey us, or are simply just being kids. This chapter is about how to share what you've learned in this book with all of the children in your life; and how to be grateful for your own children, especially when things are tough.

There are many ways to teach children about being grateful, starting at a very young age. As a former French teacher and private tutor, I have been working with children for most of my life. I love teaching and continue to teach Sunday school every week. Much of what I teach is about love, prayer and gratitude. Prayer is something that most children can understand and it's a way of showing gratitude. Simply thanking God or the Spirit for your food before you eat or at the end of the day, saying thank you for another day on this earth. Teaching children to be grateful for the clothes on their backs, the shoes on their feet, and their comfortable lifestyle also helps them to understand gratitude. I teach that not everyone has these same comforts, and that in fact many children across the globe lack the basic necessities we take for granted. They may not realize that many people don't have a home to live in, or a bed to sleep in, or food on the table at every meal.

For older children, especially teenagers, journaling can be a great way to practice being grateful. Many teenagers will have trouble sharing their emotions with their parents; offering them a safe and secret place to write it all down can help. Teach them to start each entry with at least one thing they are grateful for that day, as this can help them to feel more positive and happy.

As a family, you can do many of the exercises from the book together. Here are just a few examples:

- A vision board
- A dream book
- Goal setting
- Success list
- Clearing space

Furthermore, to help everyone in the family to become aware of their negative words and expressions, put out a jar and have everyone drop in their change when they use negative or rude language. Label the jar with a fun reward, such as "Disneyworld Fund" or "Ipad Fund". Make sure everyone buys into the reward first and then start saving!! As the contributions to the jar get smaller, change the game. Now, whenever someone says something positive (rather than negative), they add their change. Soon you'll have enough to pay for the reward.

When our kids are being difficult and trying our patience, it can be challenging to stay calm and rational. We've all had times when even though we truly, dearly, love our children, we wonder if it's possible to return them. Being a parent is difficult. And it takes **a lot** of patience. Here are a few strategies that may help you with your kids when things are tough:

- Remind yourself that there are thousands of families trying to have children, either by getting pregnant or adoption, who are still waiting.
- Take a deep breath and exhale while counting to ten before reacting in an emotional situation.
- Be grateful that (hopefully) your children are healthy.
- Keep a good memory of your child close at hand, so that when they are acting out, you can remember that this isn't always the way they are.

My personal favorite strategy is to tell myself that *this too shall pass*. Everything is a phase that does eventually pass. And every parent will agree that our kids grow up too quickly. Do your best to stay in the moment and even during the worst times, breathe and open your heart. Let love flow from your heart to your child. Allow them to learn how to diffuse anger and frustration with love and gratitude when you lead by example.

Your Turn to Take Action, Day 29:

Tell your kids you love them! Pick up the phone if you have to. You can never say it too many times. Share with them why you are grateful to be their parent. Connect with your own parents and let them know why you are grateful for them and tell them you love them too. Should you find yourself going through a difficult time with your children or your parents, use any of the strategies in this book to change your life and your attitude, and chances are the changes you make will help heal some of your relationships along the way.

Day 30—A Lifetime of Learning and Gratitude

Congratulations! You've made it to Day 30. By now, it's very likely that you've started to see some positive changes in your life. Perhaps you decided to read this book all the way through the first time, without applying any of the exercises, and that's okay! Your subconscious will have shifted simply by reading about daily gratitude, faith and abundance. Although the book is called *30 Days of Gratitude*, it will take much longer than thirty days to complete all of the exercises outlined at the end of each day. This book may be a reference for you when you feel you are slipping into a more negative mindset, or perhaps when you feel like you are ready to make a positive life change. Every time you go back to it, different chapters and exercises will stand out for you. Leave a copy on your bedside table and simply read one chapter in the evening before you go to sleep. This will help to set-up your subconscious for a good night's rest.

Every exercise in the book has value, but I'd like to highlight my top eleven favorites. If these are the only exercises you ever do, they alone will have a positive impact on your life:

1. Daily gratitude before bed each night.
2. Waking up and saying *Thank You*.
3. Reducing negative influences in your life.
4. Making your car a university on wheels.
5. Loving your body and yourself right now.
6. Creating a vision and a vision board.
7. Finding a mentor.
8. Being happy for other's successes.
9. Seeing abundance everywhere.

10. Clearing space in your life.
11. Having faith.

Remember that even small changes will make a difference in the long run. As Darren Hardy stated in *The Compound Effect*, "Consistency is the key to achieving and maintaining momentum." Choosing gratitude habits every day will soon become second nature to you. And in a few months or even a year or two, your life will be completely unrecognizable from what it was before.

Your Turn to Take Action, Day 30:

If you have yet to begin any of the gratitude habits shared in this book, pick one of the top eleven finalists. Commit to one change, starting right now. Don't wait until tomorrow, today is what counts. Just do it! Take one step towards a life full of gratitude and abundance, and I promise you won't regret it.

Epilogue

There are so many brilliant and unexpected things that have happened in my life since I started writing this book. I never expected to affect my own mindset so drastically simply by writing about gratitude. It's also been wonderful to see how my own family and friends are making changes, simply by reading the first few chapters.

One thing I know for certain, writing a book about gratitude has made me feel a whole lot more grateful every day. It is on my mind for most of the day, and I find myself checking my thoughts and actions if they are not in line with what I have been teaching in the book. Just like you, I am human and have my flaws. I am not always in a state of gratitude and have moments of negative energy as well. While writing this book, I noticed that my relationships with my daughter and husband have changed. I find that I am more patient with my two-year-old and am more grateful for the ways she is changing and growing up every day. As for my husband, I am making more of an effort to give him love and affection, and am careful not to dump negative energy on him if I'm not feeling very positive. I feel it's had a positive effect on our relationship and we are communicating better than ever before. We are also being better parents to our daughter, as we are more aligned and working better as a team.

Another relationship that has been enriched is with my sister. When she first offered to edit this book, we were both a bit unsure about how it would work. She was concerned that I would take her suggestions and edits personally and there would be a potential for conflict. After I assured her that I trusted her and was open to her feedback, the process turned into a wonderful experience for both. We have always been close, but this has been the best experience we have shared to date.

There were several books that I read while writing and editing this book, and I believe they all had an influence on shaping the outcomes. First, I read *The Untethered Soul* by Michael A. Singer. I found it to be a very powerful book, even though the writing was not always easy to follow. The underlying message is that if you choose to commit to being happy **no matter what**, you will be on your way to enlightenment. I also feel that the messages shared in *The Untethered Soul* led me to deeper understanding of some of the concepts I have shared with you.

During the editing process, I began to read Dr. Wayne Dyer's *Change Your Thoughts, Change Your Life*. Each chapter is a verse of the Tao Te Ching and Dr. Dyer's interpretation of the message. Every verse ends with an action step to complete that day. Sound familiar? As this book is meant to be read one verse per day, it was easy to reinstate my habit of reading first thing in the morning, spending ten minutes reading before giving my daughter my full attention. At the same time, I am teaching her to take a few quiet moments in the morning before turning on the television or the iPad.

In closing, I would like to thank you, dear reader, for taking some of your very precious time to make your way through the *30 Days of Gratitude* book. I am grateful for all of you. In return, my wish is that you have learned new habits, found a place for daily gratitude, and are allowing abundance into your life every single day. And when you're faced with darkness and challenges, start by opening your heart and smile, and remember that this too shall pass.

Appendix A—Recommended Reading List

Gratitude Mindset:

30 Days to Wealth—Leanne Grechulk

Excuses Begone!—Dr. Wayne Dyer

Rich Dad, Poor Dad—Robert Kyosaki

Secrets of the Millionaire Mind—T. Harv Eker

The Business of the 21st Century—Robert Kyosaki

The Challenge to Succeed—Jim Rohn (audio program)

The Greatest Salesman in the World—Og Mandino

The Law of Attraction—Michael Losier

The Magic of Thinking Big—David J. Schwartz

The Monk Who Sold His Ferrari —Robin Sharma

The Power of Your Subconscious Mind—Dr. Joseph Murphy

The Psychology of Winning—Denis Waitley

The Richest Man in Babylon—George S. Clason

The Secret—Wanda Byrne

The Seven Spiritual Laws of Success—Deepak Chopra

Think and Grow Rich—Napoleon Hill

You Were Born Rich—Bob Proctor

Gratitude and Your Healthy Body:

Accidentally Overweight—Dr. Libby Weaver

Hidden Messages in Water—Dr. Masaru Emoto

Meals that Heal Inflammation—Julie Daniluk

The New Glucose Revolution—Dr. Jennie Brand-Miller

Wheat Belly—Dr. William Davis

You Can Heal Your Life—Louise Hay

Leadership:

How to Win Friends & Influence People—Dale Carnegie
The 21 Irrefutable Laws of Leadership—John C. Maxell
The 5 Levels of Leadership—John C. Maxwell
The Compassionate Samurai—Brian Klemmer
Tribes—Seth Godin
Who Moved My Cheese?—Spencer Johnson, MD

Gratitude Habits:

The 7 Habits of Highly Effective People—Stephen R. Covey
The Compound Effect—Darren Hardy
The Greatest Secret in the World—Og Mandino
The Happiness Advantage—Shawn Achor
The Power of Focus—Jack Canfield, Mark Victor Hansen and Les Hewitt
The Success Principles—Jack Canfield
You Can Create an Exceptional Life—Louise Hay & Cheryl Richardson

Feng Shui:

Feng Shui for Prosperity—Terah Kathryn Collins
10 Minute Feng Shui—Skye Alexander

For Your Spirit:

Change Your Thoughts, Change Your Life—Dr. Wayne Dyer
The Four Agreements—Miguel Ruiz
The Power of Now —Eckhart Tolle
The untethered soul—Michael A. Singer
The Way of the Wizard—Deepak Chopra
Wishes Fulfilled—Dr. Wayne Dyer

Appendix B—Recommended Mentor List

These mentors all have a collection of books, DVDs and audio programs. I have shared my favorites in the book list. I recommend starting with one that resonates with you, and working through their body of work as you grow and learn from them.

Bob Proctor

Darren Hardy

Deepak Chopra

Denis Waitley

Dr. Wayne Dyer

Jack Canfield

Jim Rohn

John C. Maxwell

Louise Hay

Og Mandino

Robert Kyosaki

Robin Sharma

Stephen R. Covey

Appendix C—Favorite Films

Food Matters

Hungry for Change

The Secret

The Shift—Dr. Wayne Dyer

What the Bleep Do We Know?!

You Can Heal Your Life—Louise Hay

Appendix D—Worksheets

<u>30 Days of Gratitude, Day 15: A Review of the Past 12 Months</u>

Category	3 Successes	3 Areas for Improvement
Business or work	1. 2. 3.	1. 2. 3.
Family	1. 2. 3.	1. 2. 3.
Health & Fitness	1. 2. 3.	1. 2. 3.
Lifestyle	1. 2. 3.	1. 2. 3.
Spirituality	1. 2. 3.	1. 2. 3.
Education & Personal Growth	1. 2. 3.	1. 2. 3.

30 Days of Gratitude, Day 16: Creating a Yearly Plan

Category	3 Successes	3 Areas for Improvement
Business or work	1. 2. 3.	1. 2. 3.
Family	1. 2. 3.	1. 2. 3.
Health & Fitness	1. 2. 3.	1. 2. 3.
Lifestyle	1. 2. 3.	1. 2. 3.
Spirituality	1. 2. 3.	1. 2. 3.
Education & Personal Growth	1. 2. 3.	1. 2. 3.

What would it take to have your BEST year ever? What are your **3 Most Important Goals**?

4. _____

5. _____

6. _____

What is my Key Daily Behaviour for each of my **3 Most Important Goals**?

4. _____

5. _____

6. _____

Key Daily Behaviour Tracking

Specific Behaviour	M	T	W	Th	F	S	S

Made in the USA
San Bernardino, CA
15 August 2016